Formed in 1911, the Chartered Institute of Marketing is now the largest
professional marketing management body in Europe with over 24,000
members and 28,000 students located worldwide. Its primary objectives are
focused on the development of awareness and understanding of marketing
throughout UK industry and commerce and in the raising of standards of
professionalism in the education, training and practice of this key business
discipline.

# The Marketing Planner

**Malcolm H.B. McDonald**

Butterworth-Heinemann Ltd
Linacre House, Jordan Hill, Oxford OX2 8DP

 A member of the Reed Elsevier plc group

OXFORD   LONDON   BOSTON
MUNICH   NEW DELHI   SINGAPORE   SYDNEY
TOKYO   TORONTO   WELLINGTON

First published 1992
Paperback edition 1993
Reprinted 1994

© Malcolm H. B. McDonald 1992

**British Library Cataloguing in Publication Data**
McDonald, Malcolm H. B.
  The marketing planner.
  I. Title
  658.8

ISBN 0 7506 1709 8

Composition by Scribe Design, Gillingham, Kent
Printed and bound in Great Britain by Clays Ltd, St Ives plc

# Contents

# Introduction

This book is in three parts. Part I is a very brief summary of the main points of marketing planning. Part II is an actual Marketing Planning System. Part IIA operationalizes all the concepts, structures and frameworks necessary for Marketing Planning in the form of a step-by-step approach to the preparation of a Strategic Marketing Plan and an Operational Marketing Plan. In the case of the Strategic Marketing Plan, a worked example relating to each of the steps outlined is provided. The company used is the Steadfast Building Corporation. There then follows a suggested format for senior headquarters personnel who may have the task of summarising the Strategic Marketing Plans of many Strategic Business Units (SBU's) into one consolidated document. Part IIA finishes with notes on the planning timetable. Part IIB contains all the documentation necessary for you to use the Marketing Planning System in your own organization. Finally, in Part III, some examples of marketing plans are given to illustrate the main points and methodologies outlined in this book.

# PART I
# A Summary of Marketing Planning

*The purpose of marketing planning*
The purpose of marketing planning and its principal focus, are the identification and creation of competitive advantage.

*The marketing planning process*
The marketing planning *process* is simply a logical sequence of activities, leading to the setting of marketing objectives and the formulation of plans for achieving them.

*The strategic marketing plan*
The *Strategic* Marketing Plan, i.e. a plan for 3 or more years, is the intellectualization of how managers perceive their own position in their markets relative to their competitors (with competitive advantage accurately defined), what objectives they want to achieve, how they intend to achieve them (strategies), what resources are required, and what results are expected (budgets).

*The tactical operational marketing plan (1 year)*
The *Tactical* marketing plan is the detailed scheduling and costing out of the specific actions necessary for the achievement of the first year of the strategic marketing plan. The tactical marketing plan should *never* be developed before the strategic marketing plan.

*Why is marketing planning necessary?*
With increasing turbulence, complexity and competitiveness in the business environment, and the current speed of technological change, marketing planning is of vital importance for all members of successful organizations:

For *you*

- To help identify sources of competitive advantage.
- To force an organised approach.
- To develop specificity.
- To ensure consistent relationships.

*For your* superiors

● To inform.

*For* non-marketing functions

● To get support.

*For your* subordinates

● To obtain resources.
● To gain commitment.
● To set objectives and strategies.

*The principal benefits of strategic marketing planning*
1 *Greater profitability* (than non-planning companies over time).
2 *Improved productivity.*

These two benefits stem principally from:

● Systematic identification of emerging opportunities and threats.
● Specification of sustainable competitive advantage.
● Willingness and ability to meet change.
● Improved communication between executives.
● Reduction in conflicts between individuals/departments.
● Involvement of all levels of management in the process.
● More appropriate allocation of scarce resources.
● Consistency of approach throughout the organization.
● More market-focused orientation throughout the organization.

## Ten barriers to marketing planning

There are a number of barriers to effective marketing planning. The ten
principal barriers are:

● Confusion between marketing tactics and strategy.
● Difficulty isolating the marketing function from operations.
● Confusion between the marketing function and the marketing concept.
● Organizational barriers – for instance, the tribal mentality that can
  arise because of the failure to define Strategic Business Units (SBUs)
  correctly.
● Lack of in-depth analysis.
● Confusion between process and output.
● Lack of knowledge and skills.
● Lack of a systematic approach to marketing planning.

- Failure to assign priorities to objectives.
- Hostile corporate cultures.

## The 'Ten S' approach to overcoming these barriers

Figure I.1 summarizes the 'Ten S' approach to overcome each of these barriers. The sections that follow briefly elaborate each of the Ten Ss. The fundamental principles of marketing planning are provided.

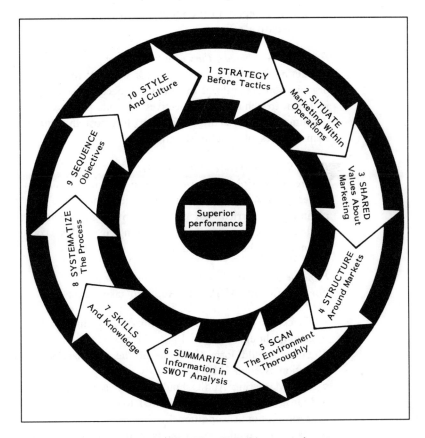

Figure I.1  *The 'Ten S' approach*

*Principle 1 – Strategy before tactics*
Develop the Strategic Marketing Plan first. This entails greater emphasis on scanning the external environment, the early identification of forces emanating from it and the development of appropriate strategic responses, bringing in all levels of management in the process.

A Strategic Plan should cover a period of between 3 and 5 years. Only when this has been developed and agreed should the 1-year Operational Marketing Plan be developed.

*Never* try to write the 1-year Operational Plan first and then extrapolate from it.

*Principle 2 – Situate marketing within operations*
For the purpose of marketing planning, put marketing as close as possible to the customer. Where practicable, have both marketing and sales departments report to the same person (who should not normally be the chief executive officer).

*Principle 3 – Shared values about marketing*
Marketing is a management process whereby the resources of the whole organization are utilized to satisfy the needs of selected customer groups, in order to achieve the objectives of both parties. It is clear from this definition that marketing is first and foremost an attitude of mind, rather than a series of functional activities.

*Principle 4 – Structure around markets*
Wherever possible, organize company activities around customer groups, rather than around functional activities, and make sure that marketing planning is carried out in these Strategic Business Units (SBUs). Without excellent marketing planning in SBUs, corporate marketing planning will be of limited value.

*Principle 5 – Scan the environment thoroughly*
For an effective Marketing Audit to take place:

- Checklists of questions, customized according to level in the organization, should be agreed.
- These should form the basis of the organization's Marketing Information System (MIS).
- The Marketing Audit should be a *required* activity.
- Managers should not be allowed to hide behind vague terms such as 'poor economic conditions'.
- Managers should be encouraged to incorporate the tools of marketing in their audits, e.g. product life cycles, portfolios, and so on.

*Principle 6 – Summarize information in SWOT analyses*
Marketing Plans are often too long and detailed to be of any practical use to busy line managers, and most contain masses of data and information that rightly belong in the company's Marketing Information System or Audit, and whose inclusion in the Marketing Plan only serve to rob it of focus and impact.

By sorting, selecting and using information, you gain *intelligence*. It is the term intelligence that accurately describes the successful marketing plan.

The SWOT device (Strengths, Weaknesses, Opportunities and Threats) is potentially a very powerful analytical tool that can give impact to the ensuing assumptions, objectives, strategies and budgets. Unfortunately, it is rarely used effectively.

To be effective a SWOT must:

- Be focused on each specific segment that is of crucial importance to the organization's future.
- Summarize important and relevant aspects of the Marketing Audit.
- Be brief, interesting and concise, but intelligible.
- Focus on *key* factors only.
- List *differential* strengths and weaknesses *vis-à-vis* competitors, focusing on competitive advantage.
- List *key* external opportunities and threats only.
- Identify and pin down the *real* issues. It should not be a list of unrelated points.
- Enable the reader to grasp instantly the main thrust of the business, even to the point of being able to write Marketing Objectives.
- Answer the implied question 'which means that ...' to determine the real implications.

*Principle 7 – Skills and knowledge*
It is vital that all those responsible for marketing in SBUs have the necessary marketing knowledge and skills for the job. In particular, they must understand and know how to use the more important tools of marketing, such as:

- *Information:*

  – how to get it.
  – how to use it.

- *Positioning:*

  – market segmentation studies.
  – Ansoff Matrix.

- *Product life cycle analysis:*

  – Gap Analysis.

- *Portfolio management:*

  - The Boston Matrix.
  - The Portfolio Summary Matrix.
  - Product.

- *Four Ps' management:*

  - Price.
  - Place.
  - Promotion.

Additionally, marketing personnel require communication and interpersonal skills.

Do not worry if some of these terms are unfamiliar, they will be explained later in this book.

*Principle 8 – Systematize the process*
Ensure that all data-collection and planning activities are systematized effectively. In this way the planned process becomes a legitimate part of the organizational fabric, as opposed to an *ad hoc* arrangement.

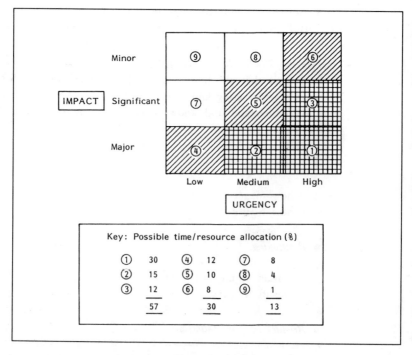

Figure I.2  *Objectives priority matrix*

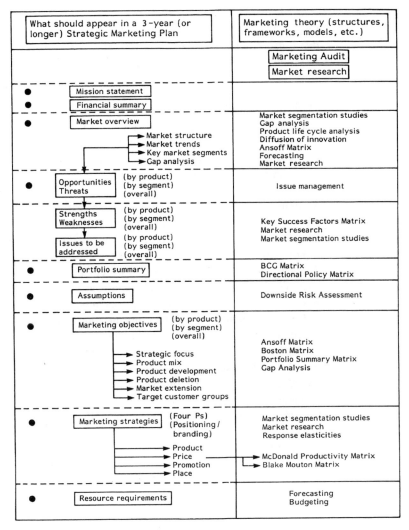

Figure I.3 *Marketing planning and marketing theory*

It is essential to have a set of written procedures and a well-argued common format for marketing planning. The purposes of such a system are:

- To ensure that all key issues are systematically considered.
- To pull together the essential elements of the strategic planning of each SBU in a consistent manner.
- To help corporate management to compare diverse businesses and to understand the condition of, and prospects for, the organization.

*Principle 9 – Sequence objectives*
Ensure that all objectives are prioritized according to their impact on the organization and their urgency, and that resources are allocated accordingly. A suggested method for prioritization is given in Figure I.2.

*Principle 10 – Style and culture*
Marketing planning will not be effective unless it has the active support and participation of the culture leaders. But even with their support, the type of marketing planning has to be appropriate for the phase of the organization's life. This phase should be measured before attempting to introduce marketing planning.

A summary of what appears in a strategic marketing plan and a list of the principal marketing tools, techniques, structures, frameworks and models that apply to each step are given in Figure I.3.
   You can see from the foregoing principles that marketing planning has never been just the simple step-by-step approach described so enthusiastically in most prescriptive texts and courses. The moment an organization embarks on the marketing planning path, it can expect to encounter a number of complex organizational, attitudinal, process and cognitive problems that are likely to block progress. By being forewarned about these barriers, there is a good chance of successfully using the step-by-step Marketing Planning System given in Part II of this manual, and of achieving excellent marketing planning, which will bring all the claimed benefits, including a significant impact on profitability, through the creation of competitive advantage. If the barriers are ignored, however, marketing planning will remain the Cinderella of business management.

# PART IIA
# A Step-By-Step Marketing Planning System

This marketing planning system is in two parts.

Part IIA takes you through a step-by-step approach to the preparation of a strategic marketing plan and a 1-year operational marketing plan. It then provides an example to show how senior headquarters' personnel can consolidate the strategic marketing plans of several SBUs into a single unified plan. Finally, the planning timetable is described.

Part IIB is concerned with documentation. Here you will find all the forms you need to prepare your own strategic and operational marketing plans.

# Introducing the Marketing Planning System

## Part IIA Planning steps

Let us begin by defining a Strategic Business Unit. A SBU will:

- Have common segments and competitors for most of its products.
- Be a competitor in an external market.
- Be a discrete and identifiable unit.
- Have a manager who has control over most of the areas critical to success.

SBUs are not necessarily the same as operating units and the definition should, if necessary, be applied all the way down to a particular product or customer, or group of products and customers.

There are four main steps in the planning process (presented in diagrammatic form in Figure II.1) that any SBU interested in protecting and developing its business must carry out:

1 *Analyse the market*. It must analyse both its market-place and its own position within it relative to the competition.
2 *Set objectives*. It must set realistic quantitative marketing and financial objectives, consistent with those set by the organization.
3 *Determine strategy*. It must determine the broad strategy that will accomplish these objectives, while conforming with the organization's corporate strategy.
4 *Formulate tactics*. It must draw together the analysis, the objectives and the strategy, using them as the foundation for detailed tactical action plans, capable of implementing the strategy and achieving the agreed objectives.

This process is formally expressed in two marketing plans – the strategic marketing plan and the tactical marketing plan – which should be written in accordance with the format provided in this system. It is designed to enable SBUs to take a logical and constructive approach to planning for success.

Two very important introductory points should be made about the strategic marketing plan:

- *Importance of different sections*. In the final analysis, the strategic marketing plan is a plan for *action* – and this should be reflected in the finished document. The implementation part of the strategic plan is represented by the subsequent 1-year Marketing Plan.

● *Length of analysis section.* To be able to produce an action-focused strategic marketing plan, a considerable amount of background information and statistics needs to be collected, collated and analysed. An analytical framework has been provided in the forms, included in the database section of the 'Strategic Marketing Plan – Documentation', which each SBU should complete. However, the commentary given in the strategic marketing plan should provide the main findings of the analysis rather than a mass of raw data. It should compel concentration upon *only* that which is essential. The analysis section should, therefore, provide just a *short* background.

## Basis of the marketing planning system

Each SBU in the organization will have different levels of opportunity, depending on the prevailing business climate. Each SBU, therefore, needs to be managed in a way that is appropriate to its own unique circumstances. At the same time, however, the chief executive officer of the SBU must have every opportunity to see that the ways in which they are managed are consistent with the strategic aims of the organization.

This system sets out the procedures that, if adhered to, will assist in achieving these aims.

Part II A sets out the marketing planning format and explains how each of the planning steps should be carried out. It explains simply and clearly what should be presented, and when, in both the 3-year strategic marketing plan and the more detailed 1-year operational marketing plan. A summary of these details is provided in Figure II.2.

The following sections explain how each of the steps in the planning process should be completed.

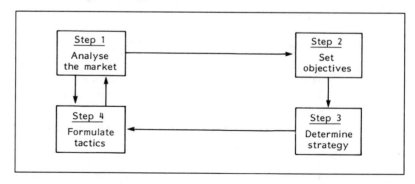

Figure II.1   *The four-step planning process*

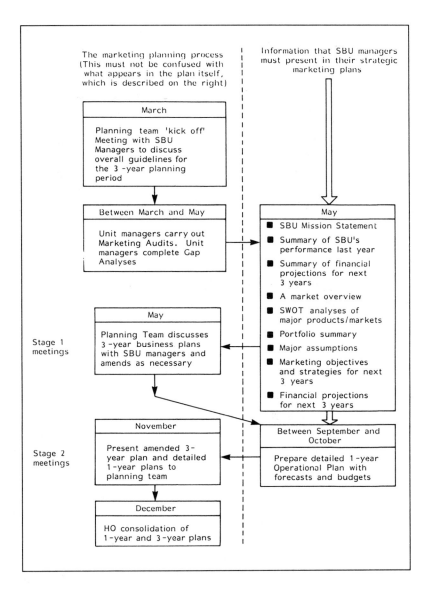

Figure II.2 *Marketing planning format. For the sake of simplicity it has been assumed that the organization's year runs from January to December. Simply amend the dates, if necessary, to suit your own organizations's timetable*

# The Marketing Audit

This audit is for completion between March and May each year but *not* for inclusion in the Strategic Marketing Plan.

Every market includes a wide variety of customer groups, not all of which will necessarily provide SBUs with opportunities for servicing profitably. In order to study those areas of the market that are potentially most favourable to the SBU's operations, it is necessary to divide the market into different *market segments* (hereafter referred to simply as segments) and to analyse sales potential by type of product within each segment. All SBUs must, therefore, analyse and evaluate the key segments in their market, plus any other segments that have been identified and selected as being of importance to them.

For the purpose of a Marketing Planning System, it is common practice to provide users with an agreed list, so that all participating SBUs employ a similar nomenclature for products and markets. We provide an example of key industrial market segments, marine market segments, and industrial product groups below:

KEY INDUSTRIAL MARKET SEGMENTS
Primary metal manufacture
Transportation equipment manufacture
General mechanical engineering/fabricated metal products
Glass and ceramics:
    Glass
    Glassware
    Refractory goods
    Ceramic goods
Road passenger and freight transportation (specialists
Truck and construction equipment distributors
Building and construction
Forestry and timber
Mining and quarrying
Food, beverage, tobacco
    Processing and manufacture
Oil and gas:
    Extraction and processing of mineral oil and natural gas, excluding off-shore, which is covered in key Marine Market Segments
Electricity: power generation and transmission

Bricks and cement:
   Manufacture of non-metallic mineral products, excluding glass and ceramics
Textiles:
   Textile industry and the production of synthetic fibres
Leather
Pulp and paper
National defence
Central and local government
   Excludes national defence
Aviation
   Excludes military aviation and aerospace manufacturing industries
Industrial distributors
   Wholesale distribution of industrial machinery, industrial spare parts and tools, etc.
Rubber, chemicals, plastics, cosmetics and pharmaceuticals

KEY MARINE MARKET SEGMENTS
*International Vessels Greater than 4000 GRT*
   Oil tankers
   LPG and chemical tankers
   Containers
   General cargo vessels
   Bulk carriers
   Ferries and roll-on/roll-off vessels
   Miscellaneous vessels
*Coastal/International Vessels Less than 4000 GRT*
   Oil tankers
   LPG and chemical tankers
   Containers
   General cargo vessels
   Bulk carriers
   Ferries and roll-on/roll-off vessels
   Miscellaneous vessels
*Fishing*
*Offshore Industry*
   Drilling rigs
   Submersibles
   Work units
*Miscellaneous*
   Harbour craft
   Inland waterways vessels
   Dredgers
   Military vessels

## INDUSTRIAL PRODUCT GROUPS

*Automotive Products*
Engine oils
Transmission fluids and gear oils
Brake fluids
Antifreeze/coolants
Greases
Miscellaneous 'others'

*Metalworking Products*
Cutting oils (soluble)
Cutting oils (neat)
Rolling oils
Other forming processes
Heat treatment

*Surface-Treatment Products*
Corrosion preventives
Non-destructive testing materials
Industrial cleaning chemicals

*General Industrial Lubricants*
Hydraulic – fire resistant
           – other
Gear oils
Turbine oils
Heat transfer oils
Compressor oils (including refrigerator)
Grease
Circulating oils
Others, e.g. wire rope lubricants, SMRs

*Aviation Lubricants*
Engine oils
Transmission oils
Hydraulic oils
Grease
Others

*Other Products*
Electrical oils
Process oils
Textile oils
Leather chemicals
Laundry and dry-cleaning chemicals
Mould releasants
Petroleum jelly
Defoamers
Others

More detailed criteria for market segmentation should also be used, where appropriate. For example: company size; geographical location; company organization, e.g. centralized or decentralized; purchasing patterns, e.g. price sensitivity, fixed annual budget, local autonomy, etc.; integration level; sales channel preference; support requirements; and so on.

A detailed description of how to conduct a Marketing Audit is contained in *Marketing Plans: How to Prepare Them; How to Use Them*, by Malcolm H.B. McDonald, published by Butterworth-Heinemann, 1989.

In summary, a Marketing Audit is a structured approach to the collection and analysis of information and data in the complex business environment, as an essential prerequisite to the preparation of the Strategic Marketing Plan.

The topics that the Marketing Audit should consider are shown in Table II.1.

Table II.1 The marketing audit

| External audit<br>*The business environment*<br>*(past, present, future)* | Internal audit<br>*Marketing operational variables*<br>*(past, present, future)* |
| --- | --- |
| **Economic environment**<br>Economic<br>Political<br>Fiscal<br>Social<br>Business<br>Legal<br>Technological<br>International<br>Intra-company<br>**The market environment**<br>Total market<br>Segments<br>Channels<br>Products<br>End use<br>Geography<br>Needs<br>Tastes<br>Habits<br>Attitudes<br>Purchasing ability<br>Stocks<br>Turnover<br>Profits | **Own company**<br>Sales (total, by geographical location, by industrial type, by customer, by product)<br>Market shares<br>Profit margins<br>Marketing mix variables, as follows:<br>● Market research<br>● Product development<br>● Product range<br>● Product quality<br>● Unit of sale<br>● Stock levels<br>● Distribution<br>● Dealer support<br>● Pricing, discounts, credit<br>● Packaging<br>● Samples<br>● Exhibitions<br>● Selling<br>● Sales aids<br>● Point of sale<br>● Advertising<br>● Sales promotion<br>● Public relations<br>● After-sales service<br>● Training |

It is appreciated that the basic information required for this Marketing Audit may not all be readily available. Nevertheless, an analysis and evaluation of the SBU's situation in each of the selected segments, i.e. a marketing audit, will provide the basis from which objectives can be set and plans prepared.

Each manager carrying out a marketing audit should complete it using internal sales data and the SBU Marketing Information System. It is helpful at this stage if the various SBU managers can issue to any subordinates engaged in the audit a market overview covering major industry and market trends. The audit will inevitably require considerably more data preparation than is necessary in the Marketing Plan itself. Therefore, all managers should start a *running reference file* for their area of responsibility during the year; this can also be used as a continual reference source and for verbal presentation of proposals.

It is essential to stress that the audit, which will be based on the running reference file, is not a marketing plan and *under no circumstances* should voluminous documents relating to the audit appear in any business plans.

# Strategic marketing plans: Sections 1–9

These sections describe what should be presented in Strategic Marketing Plans. They should be completed by the end of May each year.

These sections contain instructions to enable you to develop a Marketing Plan, together with detailed illustrative examples.

In order to make sense of the examples provided, it will be useful for you to understand something of the background of the Steadfast Building Corporation (SBC), a long-established and successful building company in the UK that originated in the Midlands. Its head office is in Birmingham and it has three regional offices: Birmingham (Midlands), Stockport (North and Scotland) and Basingstoke (South). It operates in five main building markets: industrial, offices, retail, private residential and leisure (hotels and sports centres).

Owing to the nature of its business, SBC deals with a wide range of customers, including large public limited companies, banks, building societies, pension funds, local authorities, housing associations and property developers.

The actual documentation for you to use to create your own Strategic Marketing Plans is provided in Part IIB.

## 1 SBU mission statement

*This is the first item to appear in the marketing plan.* Its purpose is to ensure that the *raison d'être* of the SBU is clearly stated. Brief statements should be made to cover the following points:

- *Role or contribution of the unit.* For example, is it a profit generator, a service department, an opportunity seeker?
- *Definition of the business.* For example, what needs do you satisfy or what benefits do you provide? Don't be too specific, e.g. 'We sell milking machinery', or too general, e.g. 'We're in the engineering business'.
- *Distinctive competence.* This should be a brief statement that applies only to your specific SBU. A statement that could equally apply to any competitor is unsatisfactory.
- *Indications for future direction.* A brief statement of the principal things you would give serious consideration to, e.g. moving into a new segment.

A completed example of SBC's mission statement follows.

---

### SBU MISSION STATEMENT

#### Steadfast Building Corporation

(i) *Role or contribution of the unit*

We aim to achieve a return on capital on funds and a growth rate which will establish us among the top six companies in our field, in the UK, using return on investment and growth as measures of success. In order to achieve this we will have to:

- Fully utilize the skills, experience and resources at our disposal.
- Ensure that employment policies, work environment and career prospects are motivating and encourage hard work, good communications, creativity, honesty and a sense of fun and excitement.

(ii) *Definition of the business*

Our business is to manage the capital investment of private and government funds in the creation of buildings and structures that meet business and/or social needs.

We achieve this in a way that reduces uncertainty and risk for our clients and leaves a quality construction as a monument to our collaboration.

(iii) *Distinctive competence*

We offer a consistent nationwide building service with a record of high standards in terms of meeting clients' needs and completing projects on time, within the agreed cost and quality specifications.

We intend to retain and enhance our reputation by continuing to be open to new ideas and technology whenever they can be harnessed to our advantage.

(iv) *Indications for future direction*

We plan to remain a dominant force in the UK construction market by exploiting new market segments which offer good commercial prospects and are compatible with our business strengths, and withdrawing from those less suited to our expertise or which offer reduced financial rewards.

---

The SBU mission statement can be presented on Form 1 in Part IIB (p. 65).

## 2 Summary of SBU's performance

This section is designed to give a bird's eye view of the SBU's total marketing activities. In addition to a quantitative summary of performance (Table II.2), SBU managers should give a written summary of what they believe to be the reasons for good or bad performance.

Table II.2   Summary of SBU's performance

|  | Three years ago | Two years ago | Last year | Current year |
|---|---|---|---|---|
| Volume/turnover (£m) | 31.2 | 38.4 | 57.5 | 84.0 |
| Gross profit ($\frac{margin}{turnover}$) (%) | 10.25 | 9.6 | 11.8 | 13.0 |
| Gross margin (turnover - costs) (£m) | 3.2 | 3.7 | 6.8 | 12.6 |

<u>Summary of reasons for good or bad performances</u>

The poor performance 2 years ago can be attributed mainly to the redefining of our markets and subsequent reorganization.  This upheaval is now behind us and we are in good shape for the future.

The summary of SBU's Performance can be filled in on Form 2 in Part IIB (p. 66).

# 3 Summary of financial projections

*This is the third item to appear in the marketing plan*, although obviously it cannot be completed until all the other procedures outlined in this manual have been completed. Its purpose is to summarize, for the person reading the plan, the financial implications over the full 3-year planning period.

It should be presented as a simple diagram and be followed by a brief commentary, as shown below for SBC (Figure II.3).

Use constant revenue ($t$) so that the projections are meaningful. '$t$' means the current year forecast; 'constant revenue' simply means that you should use the same base year values ($t$) and ignore inflation, so that you are comparing like with like.

The Summary of Financial Projections can be presented on Form 3 in Part IIB (p. 67).

Next we explain how to carry out the strategic planning gap analysis, which uses Form 4 in Part IIB (p. 68). While this need not actually appear in the marketing plan, it is none the less recommended that it is completed *before* getting into the detail of the Marketing Plan itself. It is also recommended that the results of this exercise should be agreed with your manager/director before proceeding any further.

Please note that the 'objective' point should be (as a minimum) the point that will enable you to achieve the corporate objectives set for the SBU. *Ideally, however, it should be set at a point that will make this SBU the best of its kind amongst comparable competitive SBUs.*

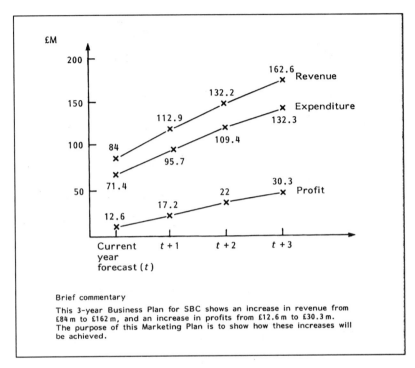

Figure II.3  *Summary of financial projections*

### Strategic planning gap analysis

Steps 1 to 6 below describe how to complete a Strategic Gap Analysis. This is followed by the actual figures generated by SBC using this process.

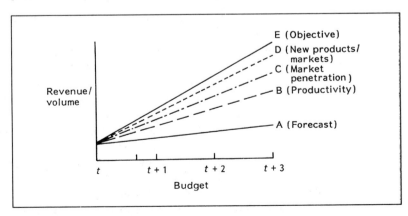

Figure II.4  *Gap analysis*

*1 Objective*
(a) Mark your current sales position at *t* (Figure II.4).
(b) Plot the sales position that you wish to achieve at the end of the planning period – point E. This is your objective.
(c) Then plot the position that you forecast you will achieve – point A.

*2 Gap analysis–productivity*
Can you close the gap by taking any of the actions listed in Table II.3? Fill in the value of each action that you consider possible on the right-hand side of the table. Calculate the total value and plot it on the Gap Analysis graph in Step 1 – this is point B.
   Steps 1 and 2 represent cash and margin focus. Now proceed to Step 3.

*Table II.3* Possible ways to close gap

| Action | Value/volume |
|---|---|
| Improve product mix<br>Make more sales calls<br>Make better sales calls<br>Increase price<br>Reduce discounts<br>Charge for deliveries<br>Others | |
| Total | |

*3 Gap analysis (2) – Ansoff product/market matrix (market penetration)*
(a) List your principal products along the top of the matrix and your principal markets down the left-hand side. In each small square write in the current sales on the left and sales achievable during the planning period on the right.
(b) Now plot the market penetration position on the Gap Analysis graph – point C. (See Figure II.5.) This is found by adding all the values in the right-hand halves of the small boxes.
   If there is still a gap, proceed to Step 4.

*4 Gap analysis (3) – Ansoff product/market matrix (new products, new markets)*
List the value of any new products that you might develop to sell to existing markets. Alternatively, or in addition, list the value of any existing products that you might sell to new markets. Add together all these values and plot the total on the gap analysis graph – this is point D. (See Figure II.6.) If there is still a gap, proceed to Step 5.

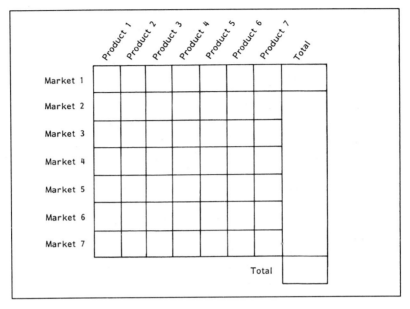

Figure II.5  *Market penetration*

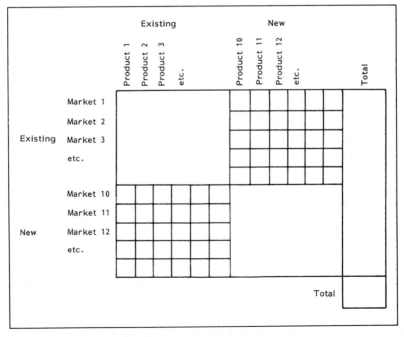

Figure II.6  *Ansoff product/market matrix*

5 *Gap analysis (4)*
Finally, list the values of any new products that you could develop for new markets until point E is reached.

Steps 3, 4 and 5 represent a sales growth focus.

6 *Changing the asset base*
If none of this enables you to reach the required revenue, consider changing the asset base – by means of investment, e.g. by acquiring another organization.

Step 6 represents a capital utilization process.

Form 4 in Part IIB (p. 68) should be used to carry out the strategic planning gap analysis.

When SBC followed this process, the following information was generated:

1  An objective at $t + 3$ of £162 M was set.
2  The starting position ($t$) revenue         = £84 M
3  The forecast growth at 15% p.a. to $t + 3$  = £128 M
4  Productivity arising mainly from more
   sales calls of better quality and more
   efficient customer service              = +£12 M
                                                  £140 M
5  Increased penetration, mainly in industrial,
   leisure and office building            = +£20 M
                                                  £160 M
6  Business from new markets, probably
   hospitals, needs a feasibility study in year
   1, but by $t + 3$ must be generating
   revenue                         = +£2 M

                                             TOTAL £162 M

## 4 Market overview

This section is intended to enable you to provide a brief overview of the market before focusing on particular details of individual market segments, which form the heart of the marketing plan.

This system is based upon the *segmentation* of markets, dividing these into homogeneous groups of customers, each having characteristics that can be exploited in marketing terms. *This approach is taken because it is the one that most successfully enables SBU managers to develop their markets.* The alternative, product-oriented approach is rarely appropriate, given the variation between different customer groups in the markets in which most organisations compete.

The market-segmentation approach is better for revealing both the weaknesses and the development opportunities than is an exclusively product-orientated approach.

While it is difficult to give precise instructions on how to present this section of the marketing plan, it should be possible (following completion of the marketing audit) to present a Market Overview that summarizes what SBU managers consider to be the key changes in their markets.

When completing this section, SBU managers should consider the following:

- What are the major products and markets (or segments) that are likely to be able to provide the kind of business opportunities suitable for the organization?
- How are these changing (i.e. which are growing and which are declining)?

This section should be brief and there should be some commentary by the SBU manager about what seems to be happening in his or her market.

*It is very helpful if SBU managers can present as much of this information as possible visually, e.g. bar charts, pie charts, product life cycles, etc.*

The market overview for SBC follows.

---

### MARKET OVERVIEW

1 Characteristics of our market segments:

(i) *Industrial buildings*
There is considerable growth in medium to small industrial parks in the South and in areas where heavy industry has declined. In addition, many old industrial buildings are unsuitable for high-technology industries. Prospects are good in this segment.

(ii) *Office building*
In most urban renewal programmes there is considerable scope for office building. Also, property developers can tap rich pension funds and investment houses. This is another good prospect area.

(iii) *Retail*
This has been a considerable growth area, with the rise in popularity of shopping precincts either in or out of towns. There is the possibility of growth slowing down as major retail chains rethink their strategies during this period of high interest rates.

*continued*

---

(iv) *Leisure*

There is still a short-fall in hotel rooms for business and tourism. Similarly, more health and recreation centres are required to meet projected lifestyle needs. These will either be provided privately or by local authorities; either way, prospects for us are good.

(v) *Residential housing*

The demand for first-time housing remains high, but green-field development opportunities are reducing in areas of high population. We need large projects to separate ourselves from small local builders who could not tackle anything on such a scale. This segment is beginning to look less attractive unless we position ourselves more creatively by redefining our markets.

2 Share of income by sector in relation to the market. See Figure II.7.

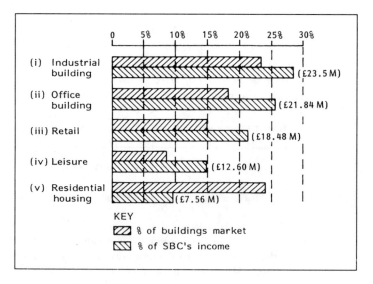

Figure II.7 *Income in relation to market share*

Total income is £84 M (current year) and income per segment is given in parentheses.

Figure II.7 shows that SBC's income per segment is relatively greater than the proportionate market breakdown in all segments except residential housing. Here much of the building has been on sites that were uneconomic for us. While this explains the apparent poor performance, it also raises questions about whether or not we should remain in this segment.

*continued*

3 Income per segment compared with market growth. See Table II.4.

Table II.4  Income compared with market growth

| Segment | Last year (£m) | Current year (£m) | Change (%) | Total market growth (%) |
|---|---|---|---|---|
| Industrial | 12.40 | 23.52 | + 90 | 24 |
| Office | 12.20 | 21.84 | + 79 | 18 |
| Retail | 15.00 | 18.48 | + 23 | 15 |
| Leisure | 9.60 | 12.60 | + 31 | 8 |
| Residential | 8.30 | 7.56 | − 9 | 24 |
| Total | 57.50 | 84.00 | + 46 | |

Once again the disappointing feature is the performance in residential housing. Our income percentage increase in all other segments far exceeds their growth rate.

4 Distribution of current-year income by customer. See Table II.5. Customer base is 260.

Table II.5  Income distribution by customers

| | Customers (%) | | | | | | | | | |
|---|---|---|---|---|---|---|---|---|---|---|
| | 10 | 20 | 30 | 40 | 50 | 60 | 70 | 80 | 90 | 100 |
| Cumulative income | 58.3 | 74.5 | 83.6 | 89.6 | 93.6 | 96.3 | 98.0 | 99.1 | 99.8 | 100 |
| Income per 10% | 58.3 | 16.2 | 9.1 | 6.0 | 4.1 | 2.6 | 1.7 | 1.1 | 0.7 | 0.2 |
| Grade | A | | B | C | | D | | | E | |

This approximates to the conventional Pareto distribution with 20 per cent of our largest customers accounting for 74.5 per cent of our total income. The customer grading bands are somewhat arbitrary, but do none the less give a good indication of when we should conduct further customer analysis.

Form 5 in Part IIB (p. 72) should be used to supply the market overview.

## 5 SWOT analyses of major products/markets

To decide on marketing objectives and future strategy, it is first necessary to summarize the SBU's *present* position in its market(s). This was done in the previous section.

With respect to the major products and markets (or segments) highlighted in the previous section, the Marketing Audit must now be summarized in the form of a number of *SWOT* analyses. *SWOT* is an acronym derived from the words *Strengths, Weaknesses, Opportunities* and *Threats*. In simple terms:

- What are the opportunities?
- What are the present and future threats to the SBU's business in each of the segments that have been identified as important?
- What are the unit's *differential* strengths and weaknesses *vis-à-vis* competitors? In other words, why should potential customers in the target markets prefer to deal with your organization rather than with your competitors?

The market overview in Section 4 will have identified what you consider to be the key products or markets (or segments) on which you intend to focus. *For presentation purposes, it is helpful if you can present a brief SWOT analysis for each of these key products or market segments.* Each SWOT analysis should be brief and interesting to read. *Complete SWOT analyses only for the key segments.*

*5.1 Some important factors for success in this business – critical success factors (strengths and weaknesses)*

How does a competitor wishing to provide products in this segment succeed? There are always relatively few factors that determine success. Factors such as product performance, breadth of services, speed of service, low costs, and so on, are often the most important factors for success.

You should now make a brief list of your organization's *strengths and weaknesses* and examine how these relate to the most important factors for success that you have identified for a particular segment. To do this, you will probably wish to consider other suppliers to the same segment in order to identify why you believe your organization can succeed and what weaknesses must be addressed in the 3-year planning period.

*Table II.6* Critical Success Factors (CSFs)

| Critical success factors | Weighting factor | Your organization | Competitor A | Competitor B | Competitor C |
|---|---|---|---|---|---|
| CSF 1<br>CSF 2<br>CSF 3<br>CSF 4 | | | | | |
| Total weighted score | 100 | | | | |

It is strongly recommended that market research should be completed to ascertain the validity of both the factors themselves and the relative importance (weighting) you have assigned them.

These factors are called Critical Success Factors (CSFs). A layout such as in Table II.6 is useful.

You should weight each factor out of 100, e.g. CSF 1 = 60; CSF 2 = 25; CSF 3 = 10; CSF 4 = 5, and fill in the weightings in the appropriate column. Next, you should score yourself and each competitor out of 10 on each of the CSFs. Write down these scores in the remaining columns. Then multiply each score by the weight, and put the resulting values in parentheses after the scores out of ten.

This will give you an accurate reading of your position in each segment *vis-à-vis* your competitors. **It will also highlight which are** *the key issues that should be addressed* **in the 3-year planning period.**

*5.2 Summary of outside influences and their implications (Opportunities and Threats)*
This should include a brief statement to show how important aspects of the environment, such as technology, government policies and regulations, the economy, and so on, have influenced this segment. There will obviously be some opportunities and some threats.

*5.3 Key issues to be addressed*
A number of key issues to be addressed will emerge from 5.1 and 5.2 above.

*5.4 Assumptions, marketing objectives, marketing strategies*
Assumptions can now be made and objectives and strategies set.

It should be stressed at this point that such assumptions, objectives and strategies relate only to each particular product or market segment under consideration. These will guide your thinking when setting wider assumptions, marketing objectives and strategies later on (see Section 7 below).

Details of the SWOT analysis should be filled in on Form 6 in Part IIB (p. 73).

Some details that describe how SBC completed its SWOT analysis are given below.

---

SBC'S SWOT ANALYSIS FOR THE INDUSTRIAL
BUILDINGS MARKET

*Strengths*

\*\*\* Size and reputation of the company.
\*\*\* Experience and track record.
\*\* Nationwide coverage.

*continued*

---

** High-quality buildings and service.
*** Quality of our staff.
** Our willingness to innovate.
*** Relationships with customers.
* Computerized administrative systems.
** Our improving marketing skills.

*Weaknesses*

* Co-ordination between regional offices could be improved.
*** Shortage of key skills in some areas, e.g. Quantity Surveying and Project Management.
** Difficulty providing consistent quality nationwide when local sub-contracted labour is used.
** Recent growth means that we have recruited a number of relatively inexperienced staff in the last 2 years.
*** We have taken on some contracts with 'mismatched' customers, i.e. we did not play to our strengths.

*Note*

The more asterisks, the more important the factor listed.

*Critical success factor analysis*

In the industrial buildings market the CSFs are:

1 Completing projects on time.
2 Completing projects within budget.
3 Producing high-quality constructions.
4 Maintaining good relationships with customers.
5 Having all necessary project services in house.

Refer now to Table II.7.

*Table II.7* Critical success factor analysis

| Critical success factors | Weighting | SBC | Competitor A | Competitor B | Competitor C |
|---|---|---|---|---|---|
| 1 | 30 | 10 (300) | 10 (300) | 8 (240) | 6 (180) |
| 2 | 30 | 10 (300) | 9 (270) | 8 (240) | 7 (240) |
| 3 | 15 | 8 (120) | 10 (150) | 7 (105) | 9 (135) |
| 4 | 15 | 7 (105) | 7 (105) | 7 (105) | 7 (105) |
| 5 | 10 | 10 (100) | 7 (70) | 10 (100) | 8 (80) |
| Total weighted score | 100 | 925 | 895 | 790 | 710 |

Raw scores = 1 low → 10 high.
Weighted scores = raw score x weighting factor. These are shown in parentheses.

On a weighted comparison of the CSFs in the industrial buildings market we outscore our main competitors A, B and C.

This analysis suggests that SBC needs to work at establishing construction quality standards approaching those of competitor A, if we are to maintain our reputation.

*Opportunities*

** More foreign companies are setting up new plants in the UK.

** EEC deregulation – we must look for collaboration with a mainland partner.

*** We could extend regional coverage in the South by opening up another office.

* We could buy out small local builders to improve our 'network'.

* We could use some of our internal services, e.g. quantity surveying, JIT system, as separate profit centres, i.e. as revenue earners.

*** The continued growth in high-tech businesses with high demand for purpose-built premises, especially in the South-east.

*Threats*

*** Downturn of the economy due to continued high interest rates may lead to a recession.

** Loss of key personnel.

*** Problems of recruiting the right calibre people.

* EEC deregulation gives rise to new competition.

* Material shortages.

** Revitalized, more sophisticated competitors.

** Continued growth will overstretch SBC and lead to inefficiencies.

** The environmental lobby makes it increasingly difficult to obtain land and/or planning permission.

*Key issues to be addressed*

1 Throughout the SWOT analysis, one key issue stands out – 'staff'. Our future plans and reputation depend upon our recruiting and keeping the right calibre people. Therefore, we will have to ensure that our total 'employment package' matches the best that can be found in our industry.

2 We need to win the lion's share of all new industrial building projects for which we compete. By developing our marketing and, in particular, selling skills, by extending our presence 'on the ground' and by maintaining our current high standards of quality and completions on time, we should be well placed to win new contracts.

3 We need to ensure that new contracts are well matched to our business skills and must guard against competing for any that are not.

4 We need to monitor more closely and systematically what our main competitors are doing. Our information on them is somewhat 'patchy' at present and subject to much guesswork.

5 We need to set a timetable for our regional offices to become autonomous business units, with their own self-generated marketing plans that can more accurately reflect local conditions and opportunities.

*Assumptions*

Three main assumptions have been made:

1 The economy does not go into deep depression.
2 We maintain a similar organizational structure over the next 3 years,
   i.e. regional offices with a central co-ordinating/planning function.
3 No new competitor enters the field and makes a significant impact.

*Marketing objectives and strategies (industrial segment)*

See Table II.8

*Table II.8* Marketing objectives and strategies

| Objectives | Strategies |
| --- | --- |
| 1 Increase turnover from £25 M to £60 M | Improve market penetration and broaden customer base.* Target new customers more accurately.* Develop more business from existing high-potential customers. |
| *Note* As a safeguard, no one customer in this segment is to account for more than 10% of turnover. | |
| 2 Improve profitability from £4 M to £10 M | Eliminate mismatched, unprofitable customers in our portfolio, and concentrate our efforts on those with high profit potential. Improve inventory control and logistics. |
| 3 Explore new markets in order to obtain revenue in year *t* + 3 | Determine the potential of new markets, e.g. hospitals. Identify prospects of EEC deregulation and/or collaboration with a Euro-partner. Develop a more attractive employment package to attract new and retain existing staff. |

## 5.5 *Competitor analysis*

Here you should summarize the findings of the Audit with respect to *major competitors* only. For each competitor, you should indicate the current market share within the particular product or market segment under consideration, *and their expected share 3 years from now.* The greater a competitor's influence over others, the greater its ability to implement its own independent strategies; hence the more successful it is.

Also list their principal products or services and their principal markets.

Next, list each major competitor's business direction and current strategies. A list of business directions and strategies is given below. *These should not be quoted verbatim* – they are given only as guidelines.

Next, list each competitor's major strengths and weaknesses.

Finally, it is suggested that you should classify each of your main competitors according to one of the classifications in the guide to competitive position classification i.e. leadership, strong, favourable, tenable, weak.

The following list includes five business directions that are appropriate for almost any business. Select those that best summarize the competitor's strategy:

1 *Enter.* Allocate resources to a new business area. Consideration should include building from prevailing company or division strengths, exploiting related opportunities and defending against perceived threats. May involve creating a new industry.

2 *Improve.* Apply strategies that will significantly improve the competitive position of the business. Often requires thoughtful product/market segmentation.

3 *Maintain.* Maintain one's competitive position. Aggressive strategies may be required, although a defensive posture may also be assumed. Product/market position is maintained, often in a niche.

4 *Harvest.* Intentionally relinquish competitive position, emphasizing short-term profit and cash flow but not necessarily at the risk of losing the business in the short term. Often entails consolidating or reducing various aspects of the business to create higher performance for that which remains.

5 *Exit.* To dispose of a business because of its weak competitive position or because the cost of staying in it is prohibitive and the risk associated with improving its position is too high.

The following is a guide to competitive position classifications:

*Leadership*

● Has a major influence on performance or behaviour of other competitors.

*Strong*

● Has a wide choice of strategies.
● Is able to adopt independent strategy without endangering short-term position.
● Has low vulnerability to competitors' actions.

*Favourable*

● Exploits specific competitive strength, often in a product/market niche.

- Has more than an average opportunity to improve position; several strategies available.

*Tenable*

- Performance justifies continuation in business.

*Weak*

- Current performance is unsatisfactory; significant competitive weakness.
- Inherently a short-term condition; must improve or withdraw.

Form 7 in Part IIB (p. 74) provides a useful format for completing your competitor analysis.

SBC's competitor analysis is given in Table II.9.

*Table II.9* Competitor analysis

| Main competitor | Market share | | Products/ markets | Business directions, current objectives and strategies | Strengths | Weaknesses | Competitive position |
|---|---|---|---|---|---|---|---|
| | New | 3 years time | | | | | |
| Carpenters | | | | Maintain | Good reputation | Not an innovator. No national coverage. | Favourable |
| MacLelland | | | | Harvest | Rapid growth | Tied into some troublesome contractors. Cash-flow problems. | Tenable/ weak |
| Breezer | | | | Improve/ maintain | Good reputation. National coverage | Losing key staff to us. Very low-key image/ passive marketer. | Favourable/ strong |

Notes
1 Information on comparative market share now and in 3 years' time would be very useful, but at present is not available to us. 2 In terms of products/markets, the competitors listed and ourselves could be taken to be very similar. Therefore, we have not completed the column explaining 'Products/markets'.

# 6 Portfolio summary (summary of SWOTs)

All that remains is to summarize each of these SWOTs in a format that makes it easy to see at a glance the position and relative importance of each of these product/market segments to the organization.

This can be done by drawing a diagram in the form of a four-box portfolio, which will show each of the important product/market segments described earlier (Figure II.8).

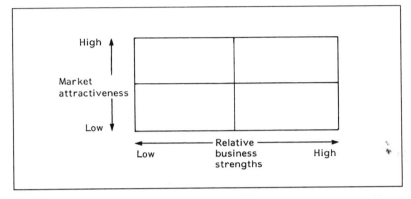

Figure II.8   *Portfolio matrix*

The portfolio matrix enables you to assess which products or services, or which groups of customers or market segments, offer the best chance of commercial success. It will also aid decision-making about which products or services (or market segments) merit investment, both in terms of finance and managerial effort.

In the example that follows, market segments are used, although it is possible to use products or services. A matrix for your use is provided as Form 8 in Part IIB (p. 75). You should transfer all the information that you gain by using the following procedure on to this worksheet.

This is the procedure we recommend that you follow to arrive at a Portfolio Matrix for your SBU.

*Procedure for arriving at your portfolio matrix*
Make a list of your market segments on a separate piece of paper and decide which ones are the most attractive. (Please note, these 'segments' can be countries, divisions, markets, distributors, customers, etc.) To arrive at these decisions you will no doubt take several factors into account. For example:

● Your organization's experience in each market.
● The size of the markets.
● Their actual or prospective growth.
● The prices you can charge.
● Profitability.

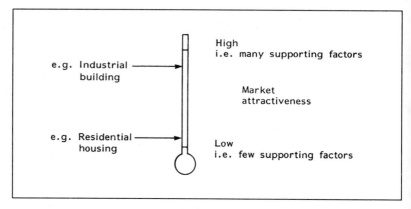

Figure II.9  *Measuring market attractiveness*

- The diversity of needs that you can meet.
- The amount of competition, in terms of quality and quantity.
- The supportiveness of the business environment.
- Technical developments.

Imagine that you have a measuring instrument, something like a thermometer, which measures not temperature but market attractiveness. The higher the reading, the more attractive the market. This instrument is shown in Figure II.9. Estimate the position of *each* of your markets on the scale and make a note of them.

Generally speaking, most organizations are concerned about the *potential* for:

- Growth in revenue or volume.
- Growth in profitability.

*Table II.10* Deciding market attractiveness

| Market attractiveness factors | Competitive position factors |
|---|---|
| • Market size | • Market share |
| • Market growth | • Profitability |
| • Competitive intensity | • 'Real need' identified/satisfied |
| • Vulnerability | • Product or service differentiation |
|   – Industry restructuring | • Product quality/value |
|   – Raw materials | • Investment intensity |
|   – Key suppliers | • Technology lead/lag |
| • Market profitability | • Market coverage |
| • Cyclicity | • Manufacturing capability/cost |
| • Regulatory influence | • Ability to protect economics as market matures |
| • Life cycle characteristics | |
| • Price sensitivity | • Company reputation or image |
| • Barriers to entry | • Labour relations climate |
| • Customer structure | • Workforce availability |

There are, however, other factors that can be considered, such as the size of the market, competitive intensity and so on. A fuller list for your consideration is given in Table II.10.

From this list, managers may select the market attractiveness and business strength factors they consider most appropriate for analysing their business. Although some of these may be relatively unimportant to a particular business, those that are printed in bold type should always at least be considered. You may add factors to this list if appropriate. Generally, the degree of complexity of the environment of the business will determine the number of factors required for your analysis, but try if possible, to keep the list to five or less.

Once the criteria for attractiveness have been agreed, you need a scoring system for each factor, and each factor should be weighted according to how important it is to you. A hypothetical worked example is shown in Table II.11.

*Table II.11*   Market attractiveness evaluation

| Factor | Scoring criteria | | | Score | Weighting (%) | Ranking |
|--------|------|------|------|-------|---------------|---------|
| | 10-7 | 6-3 | 2-0 | | | |
| Market size (£ millions) | >250 | 50-250 | <50 | 5 | 15 | 0.75 |
| Volume growth (%) | >10 | 5-10 | <5 | 10 | 25 | 2.5 |
| Competitive intensity | Low | Medium | High | 6 | 10 | 0.6 |
| Industry profitability (%) | >15 | 10-15 | <10 | 8 | 25 | 2.0 |
| Vulnerability | Low | Medium | High | 6 | 15 | 0.9 |
| Cyclicity | Low | Medium | High | 2.5 | 10 | 0.25 |
| | | | | | TOTAL | 7.0 |

The score for the market is derived by multiplying the individual score for each factor by its percentage weighting and totalling the results. The highest possible total is 10, so a score of 7 places this market in the highly attractive category.

Now put each of your listed markets through this scoring/weighting device to find their positions on the market attractiveness scale.

When you have completed this exercise, transfer this information on to the worksheet in Form 8 of 'The Strategic Marketing Plan – Documentation' (p. 75), writing your own markets on the left of the matrix, as indicated in Figure II.10. Still using the worksheet, draw a dotted line horizontally across from the top left-hand market, as shown. Now ask yourself how well is your SBU equipped to deal with this most attractive market. A whole series of questions need to be asked to establish the company's business strengths, for example:

● Are we big enough?
● Can we grow?
● How large is our market share?
● Do we have the right services?

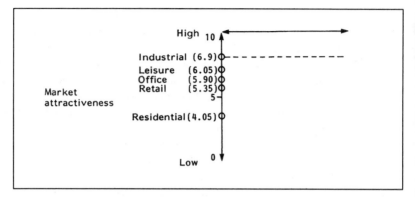

Figure II.10 *Market attractiveness*

- How well are we known in this market?
- What image do we have?
- Do we have the right technical skills?
- Can we adapt to changes?
- Do we have funds to invest if required?
- Do we have enough capacity?
- How close are we to this market?
- How do we compare with competitors?

The outcome of such an analysis will enable you to arrive at a conclusion about the 'fitness' of your SBU, and you will be able to choose a point on the horizontal scale of the matrix to represent this. The left of the scale represents many SBU strengths, the right few SBU strengths.

The analysis completed in the previous section should be used as input to this exercise, since you have already completed the necessary quantification.

However, be sure to use the *ratio* of your own score to that of your highest-scoring competitor. Thus, if your score were 4.8 and best competitor's score were 9.6, your ratio would be 0.5:1; whereas if your score were 7 and the next highest score were 6, your ratio would be 1.16:1. Thus, your own score can only be on the *left* of the central dividing line of the horizontal axis if your ratio is greater than 1. Use

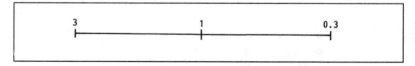

Figure II.11 *Logarithmic scale*

a logarithmic scale for the horizontal axis that goes from 0.3 to 3, as shown in Figure II.11. Draw a vertical line from the point on this scale that represents the value of your ratio, as shown, so that it intersects with the horizontal line. See Figure II.12.

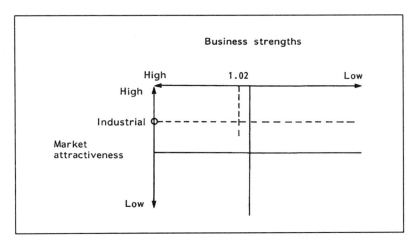

Figure II.12 *Business strengths and market attractiveness*

Now draw circles at the points where the lines intersect, this time making the diameter of each circle proportional to that segment's share of your total sales turnover. (Please note that to be technically correct you should take the square root of your sales volume, but in our view this is not essential. Now indicate where these circles will be in 3 years' time and their estimated size. The matrix may, therefore, have to show segments not currently served.

There are two ways of doing this. First, in deciding on market or segment attractiveness, you can assume that you are at year $t$, i.e. today, and that your forecast of attractiveness covers the next 3 years, i.e. until $t+3$. If this is your chosen method, then it will be clear that *the circles can only move horizontally along the axis*, as all that will change is your business strength. The second method shows the current attractiveness position on the vertical axis, based on the past 3 years, (i.e. $t-3$ to $t$, and then forecasts how that attractiveness position will change during the next three years, $t$ to $t+3$. In such a case, the circles can move both vertically and horizontally. This is the method used in the example provided, but it is entirely up to you which method you use.

It is essential to be creative in your use of the portfolio matrix. Be prepared to change the names on the axes and to experiment with both products and markets.

This is how SBC completed its portfolio matrix.

*SBC example*

At SBC it was decided that there were five criteria for market attractiveness, as shown in Table II.12. In order to introduce a means of scoring the relative merits of each market segment against these criteria, a 0–10 point scoring system was used. In addition, because the criteria were not equally important, a 'weighting factor' was used to enable a more realistic comparison to be made between the final scores.

For SBC, 'market growth' and 'profitability' were both seen to be important issues in terms of assessing market attractiveness. Accordingly, they were given a weighting factor of 25. In contrast, 'market size' was seen as less important and its weighting factor of 10 mirrors its lesser value.

Table II.12 shows the format that SBC developed. The score for each market segment was established by multiplying the individual score by its percentage weighting factor and totalling the results. Under this scoring procedure, the highest possible total score will be 100.

*Table II.12*   SBC's assessment of market attractiveness

| Attractiveness criterion | Points allocation | | | Weighting factor |
|---|---|---|---|---|
| | 0–3 points | 4–6 points | 7–10 points | |
| Market size | Low | Medium | High | 10 |
| Market growth | Negative | Static | Positive | 25 |
| Sensitivity to price | High | Medium | Low | 20 |
| Competitive activity | High | Medium | Low | 20 |
| Profitability | < 10% | 10–15% | > 15% | 25 |

Table II.13 shows what SBC found when all the segments were scored.

*Table II.13*   Results of SBC's assessment

| Segment | Total weighted score | Attractiveness ranking |
|---|---|---|
| Industrial | 690 | 1 |
| Office | 590 | 3 |
| Retail | 535 | 4 |
| Leisure | 605 | 2 |
| Residential | 405 | 5 |

Using this information, SBC constructed the vertical axis of the Portfolio Matrix in the way shown in Figure II.13.

Since the total weighted scores represented the relative market attractiveness of each segment and ranged from 405 (lowest) to 690 (highest), the mid-point on the axis was calculated to be 548. For SBC, irrespective

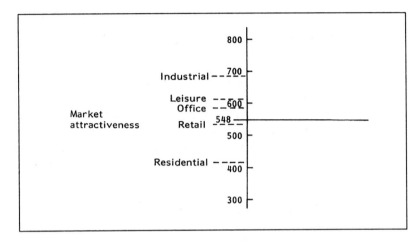

Figure II.13  *SBC assessment of market attractiveness*

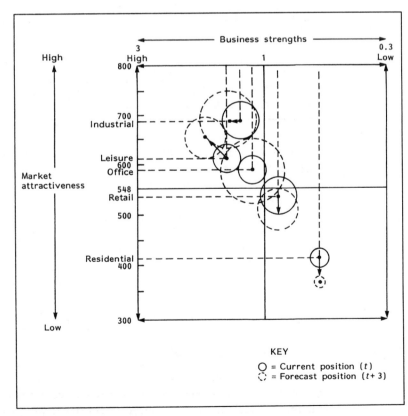

Figure II.14  *SBC's completed portfolio matrix*

of the actual scores, anything above this mid-point is becoming increasingly attractive, whereas below this line the reverse is true.

The axis was extended by one unit at each end in order to provide some space on the completed portfolio matrix.

As for relative business strengths, consider the calculations made on p. 34, using a weighted comparison of SBC *vis-à-vis* its main competitors in the industrial buildings market. Comparing SBC (score 925) with its leading competitor (score 895), the relative business strengths scores per market segment were as follows, though the data upon which these calculations were based are not provided in the text:

| | | |
|---|---|---|
| (a) | Industrial building | 1.04 |
| (b) | Office building | 1.02 |
| (c) | Retail building | 0.98 |
| (d) | Leisure building | 1.14 |
| (e) | Residential building | 0.51 |

SBC's completed portfolio matrix is shown in Figure II.14.

## 7 Assumptions

Each SBU must highlight the assumptions that are critical to the fulfilment of the planned marketing objectives and strategies.

Key planning assumptions deal in the main with outside features and anticipated changes that would have a significant influence on the achievement of marketing objectives' profitability. These might include such things as market growth rate, your organization's costs, capital investment, and so on.

Assumptions should be few in number and relate only to key issues, such as those identified in the SWOT analyses. If it is possible for a plan to be implemented irrespective of the assumptions made, then those assumptions are not necessary and should be removed.

You should find that the more-detailed lists of assumptions made for each of the principal product/market segments analysed in the SWOT stage (Section 5) will be helpful in deciding what the macro-assumptions should be.

Make a list of your assumptions on Form 9, in Part IIB (p. 76).

## 8 Setting objectives and strategies

### 8.1 Marketing objectives

Identification and statement of key strengths, weaknesses, opportunities and threats, and the explicit statement of assumptions about conditions affecting the business, make the process of setting marketing objectives

*strategic
business
unit*

easier, since they will be a realistic statement of what the SBU desires to achieve as a result of market-centred analysis. As in the case of objective-setting for other functional areas of the business, this is the most important step in the whole process, as it is a commitment on an SBU-wide basis to a particular course of action that will determine the scheduling and costing out of subsequent actions.

An *objective* is what the SBU wants to achieve; a *strategy* is how it plans to achieve it. Thus there are objectives and strategies at all levels in marketing. For example, there can be advertising objectives and strategies, pricing objectives and strategies, and so on.

However, the important point about marketing objectives is that they should concern products and markets only, since it is only by selling something to someone that the SBU's financial goals can be achieved. Advertising, pricing and other elements of the marketing mix are other means (the strategies) by which the SBU can succeed in doing this. Thus, pricing objectives, sales promotion objectives, advertising objectives and the like should *not* be confused with marketing objectives.

If profits and cash flows are to be maximized, each SBU must consider carefully how its current customer needs are changing and how the products it offers need to change accordingly. Since change is inevitable, it is necessary for SBUs to consider the two main dimensions of commercial growth, i.e. product development and market development.

Marketing objectives are concerned with the following:

- Selling existing products to existing segments.
- Developing new products for existing segments.
- Extending existing products to new segments.
- Developing new products for new segments.

Marketing objectives should be *quantitative*, and should be expressed where possible in terms of *values*, *volumes* and *market shares*. General directional terms such as 'maximize', 'minimize' and 'penetrate' should be avoided, unless quantification is included.

The marketing objectives should cover the full 3-year planning horizon and should be accompanied by broad strategies (discussed in the following section) and broad revenue and cost projections for the full 3-year period. The 1-year Marketing Plan should contain specific objectives for the first of the three-year planning cycle and the corresponding strategies that will be used to achieve these objectives. *The 1-year and 3-year plans should be separate documents. At this stage a detailed 1-year plan is not required.*

At this point it is worth stressing that the key document in the annual planning round is the 3-year strategic plan. The 1-year plan represents the specific actions that should be undertaken in the first year of the 3-year strategic plan.

### 8.2 Marketing strategies

Marketing strategies should state in broad terms *how* the marketing objectives are to be achieved, as follows:

- The specific product policies (the range, technical specifications, additions, deletions, etc.).
- The pricing policies to be followed for product groups in particular market segments.
- The customer service levels to be provided for specific market segments, such as maintenance support.
- The policies for communicating with customers under each of the main headings, such as sales force, advertising, sales promotion, etc., as appropriate.

Some of the marketing objectives and strategies available to SBU managers are summarized below.

*Objectives*
- Market penetration.
- Introduce new products to existing markets.
- Introduce existing products to new markets (domestic).
- Introduce existing products to new markets (international).
- Introduce new products to new markets.

*Strategies*
- Change product design, performance, quality or features.
- Change advertising or promotion.
- Change unit price.
- Change delivery or distribution.
- Change service levels.
- Improve manufacturing productivity.
- Improve marketing productivity, e.g. improve the sales mix.
- Improve administrative productivity.
- Consolidate product line.
- Withdraw from markets.
- Consolidate distribution.
- Standardize design, consolidate production, change sourcing.
- Acquire markets, products, facilities.

### 8.3 Guidelines for setting marketing objectives and strategies

Completing a portfolio matrix (which you have done in Section 7) for all the major products/market segments within each SBU enables you to represent graphically the characteristics of the business so that their relative positions can be clearly seen and easily understood. Additionally, each product/market segment's position on the matrix suggests broad goals that are usually appropriate for businesses in that position, although SBU managers should also consider alternative goals in the light of the special circumstances prevailing at the time.

The four categories on the matrix can be labelled as 'Stars', 'Cash cows', 'Dogs and Wildcats' (or 'Problem children', or 'Question marks'). These are the original terms coined by the Boston Consulting Group, and they have been retained here for the portfolio summary matrix. You may prefer to use your own terms, although it should be stressed that it isn't necessary to attach any particular names to each of the quadrants.

Each of these is considered in turn.

Products in the 'Star' category enjoy competitive positions in market segments characterized by high growth rates and are good for continuing attractiveness. The obvious objectives for such products are either to maintain growth rates at the market growth rate, thus maintaining market share and market leadership, or to grow faster than the market, thus increasing market share.

Three principal factors should be considered:

- Possible geographical expansion.
- Possible product line expansion.
- Possible product line differentiation.

These could be achieved by means of internal development, acquisition or joint ventures.

The main point is that in attractive marketing situations like this, *an aggressive marketing posture is required*, together with a very tight budgeting and control process to ensure that capital resources are efficiently utilized.

Products in the 'Cash cow' category enjoy competitive positions in market segments that are not considered attractive in the longer term. Here the thrust should be towards maintaining a profitable position, with greater emphasis on present earnings than on aggressive growth.

The most successful product lines should be maintained, while less successful ones should be considered for pruning. Marketing effort should be focused on differentiating products to maintain share of key segments of the market.

Discretionary marketing expenditure should be limited, especially when unchallenged by competitors or when products have matured. Comparative prices should be stabilized, except when a temporary aggressive stance is necessary to maintain market share.

'Dogs' have a poor position in unattractive markets. These products are 'bad' only if objectives are not appropriate to the company's position in the market segment. Generally, where immediate divestment is not warranted, these products should be managed for cash. Product lines should be aggressively pruned, while all marketing expenditure should be minimized, with prices maintained or where possible raised.

However, a distinction needs to be made between different types of 'dogs'. The two principal categories are: 'genuine dogs' and 'cash dogs'.

'Genuine dogs' should generally be managed as outlined above. 'Cash dogs', (i.e. products close to the 'cash cow' quadrant), should generally be managed differently. For example, the reality of low growth should be acknowledged and the temptation to grow the product at some previous high rate of growth should be resisted. A 'cash dog' should not be viewed as a marketing problem, as this would probably lead to high advertising, promotion and inventory costs, and consequently lower profitability. Growth segments should be identified and exploited where possible. Product quality should be emphasized to avoid 'commodity' competition. Productivity should be systematically improved. The attention of talented managers should be focused on 'cash dogs'.

With 'Wildcats' it is necessary to decide whether to invest for future market leadership in these attractive market segments or whether to manage for present earnings. Both objectives are feasible, but it must be remembered that managing these products for cash today is usually inconsistent with market share growth, and it is usually necessary to select the most promising wildcats and invest in them only.

*8.4 Further marketing and other functional guidelines*
Further marketing and other functional guidelines that operating unit managers should consider when setting marketing objectives and corresponding strategies are shown in Table II.14. It should be stressed, however, that there can be no *automatic* policy for a particular product or market, and SBU managers should consider three or more options before deciding on 'the best' for recommendation.

Above all, SBU managers must evaluate the most attractive opportunities and assess the chances of success in the most realistic manner possible. This applies particularly to new business opportunities, which would normally be expected to build on existing strengths, particularly in marketing, and subsequently expanded or supplemented.

*8.5 Database*
Forms 10–12 in 'The Strategic Marketing Plan – Documentation' should be used to fill in Database details (see pp. 77–8).

The forms included in the Database provide both an analytical framework and a summary of marketing objectives that are relevant to all SBU managers:

*Table II.14* Other functional guidelines suggested by the portfolio summary matrix analyses

| | STAR | CASH COW | CASH DOG | DOG | WILD-CAT |
|---|---|---|---|---|---|
| Main thrust | Invest for growth | Maintain market position Manage for earnings | | Manage for cash | Opportunistic development |
| Market share | Maintain or increase dominance | Maintain or slightly milk for earnings | Maintain selectively Segment | Forgo share for profit | Invest selectively in share |
| Products | Differentiation, line expansion | Prune less successful, differentiate for key segments | Emphasize product quality Differentiate | Aggressively prune | Differentiation, line expansion |
| Price | Lead Aggressive pricing for share | Stabilize or raise | Maintain or raise | Raise | Aggressive pricing for share |
| Promotion | Aggressive marketing | Limit | Maintain selectively | Minimize | Aggressive marketing |
| Distribution | Broaden distribution | Hold wide distribution pattern | Segment | Gradually withdraw distribution | Limited coverage |
| Cost control | Tight control Go for scale economies | Emphasize cost reduction, viz. variable costs | Tight control | Aggressively reduce both fixed and variable | Tight, but not at expense of entrepreneurship |
| Production | Expand, invest (organic, acquisition, joint venture) | Maximize capacity utilization | Increase productivity, e.g. specialization, automation | Free up capacity | Invest |
| R & D | Expand, invest | Focus on specific projects | Invest selectively | None | Invest |
| Personnel | Upgrade management in key functional areas | Maintain Reward efficiency Tighten organization | Allocate key managers | Cut back organization | Invest |
| Investment | Fund growth | Limit fixed investment | Invest selectively | Minimize and divest opportunistically | Invest |
| Working capital | Reduce in process, extend credit | Tighten credit, reduce accounts receivable, increase inventory turn | Reduce | Aggressively reduce | Invest |

- *Form 10 – Market Segment Sales Values*, showing, across a 5-year period, total market demand, the SBU's own sales and the market share these represent for the various market segments.
- *Form 11 – Market Segment Gross Profits*, showing, across a 5-year period, the SBU's sales value, gross profit and gross margin for the various market segments.
- *Form 12 – Product Group Analysis*, showing, across a 5-year period, the SBU's sales value, gross profit and gross margin for different product groups.

Although these forms were completed by SBC, it has been decided not to include such detail.

*8.6 Summary of main marketing objectives and strategies*
You should now make a list of your main marketing objectives. Remember, marketing objectives are about what is sold and to whom, and should be quantitative, e.g. market share, volume, value, profit, outlet penetration.

Proceed from here to explain (usually under the 'Four Ps' headings) the principal ways in which these objectives will be achieved.

Form 13 in Part IIB (p. 79) can be used to provide this summary. SBC's summary follows.

*SBC example*

The main objective for the next 3 years is to consolidate and improve our position in the UK building market by increasing our revenue from £84M to £162M and maintaining a growth rate which is as good or better than the top five competing companies.

Principle sub-objectives are:

1 To reduce our commitment to the residential housing market from £7.5M to £5M.
2 To increase our penetration of the industrial market and increase revenue from £23.5M to £60M.
3 To develop our presence in the leisure market by more aggressive selling and promotion, increasing revenue from £12.5M to £25M.
4 Etc. etc.

## 9 Financial projections for 3 years

Finally, SBU managers should provide projections for the full 3-year planning period under all the principal standard revenue and cost headings as specified by your organization.

These details are not provided here for SBC.

Financial Projections for Three Years can be filled in on Form 14 in Part IIB (p. 80).

# The 1-year operational marketing plan

This plan should be kept separate from the 3-year Strategic Marketing Plan and should not be completed until the planning team has approved that plan in May each year.

Specific sub-objectives for products and segments, supported by more detailed strategy and action statements, should now be developed. *Budgets* and *targets*, and a *consolidated budget*, should be included here. These must reflect the marketing objectives and strategies, and in turn the objectives, strategies and programmes *must* reflect the agreed budgets and sales forecasts. Their main purposes are to delineate the major steps required in implementation, to assign accountability to focus on the major decision points, and to specify required allocation of resources and their timing.

If the procedures in this system are followed, a hierarchy of *objectives* will be built up in such a way that every item of budgeted expenditure can be related directly back to the initial financial objectives (this is known as task-related budgeting). Thus when, say, advertising has been identified as a means of achieving an objective in a particular market, i.e. advertising is a strategy to be used, all advertising expenditure against items appearing in the budget can be related back specifically to a major objective. The essential feature of this is that budgets are set against both the marketing objectives and the sub-objectives for each element of the marketing mix.

The principal advantage is that this method allows operating units to build up an increasingly clear picture of their markets.

This method of budgeting also allows every item of expenditure to be fully accounted for as part of an objective approach. It also ensures that when changes have to be made during the period to which the plan relates, such changes can be made in a way that causes the least damage to the SBU's long-term objectives.

*Guidelines for completion of the 1-year Marketing Plan*

Because of their varying nature, it is impossible to provide a standard format for all SBUs. There is, however, a minimum amount of information that should be provided to accompany the financial documentation between September and October. There is no need to supply market background information, as this should have been completed in the 3-year Strategic Marketing Plan.

*Suggested format for the 1-year marketing plan*
*Objectives.* These should cover the following:

- Volume – last year, current year estimate, budget next year.
- Invoicing (value) – last year, current year estimate, budget next year.
- Gross margins – last year, current year estimate, budget next year.

Against each there should be a few words of commentary or explanation.

*Strategies.* For example, new customers, new products, advertising, sales promotion, selling, customer service, pricing.

Objectives and strategies can be detailed on Forms A and B in Part IIB (pp. 81 and 82).

*Sub-objectives.* More detailed objectives should be provided for products, markets, market segments or major customers, as appropriate.

The strategies by which sub-objectives will be achieved should be stated. The details, timing, responsibility and cost should also be stated.

Sub-objectives can be detailed on Form C in Part IIB (p. 82).

*Summary of marketing activities and costs.* See Form D in Part IIB (p. 83).

*Contingency plan.* It is important to include a Contingency Plan, which should address the following questions:

- What are the critical assumptions on which the 1-year plan is based?
- What would the financial consequences be, i.e. the effect on the operating income, if these assumptions were incorrect? For example, if a forecast of revenue is based on the assumption that a major customer will decide to buy new plant, what would the effect be if that customer did not go ahead?
- How will these assumptions be managed?
- What action will you take to ensure that the adverse financial effects of an unfulfilled assumption are mitigated, so that your result at the end of the year is as forecast?

To measure the risk, assess the negative or down side, asking what can go wrong with each assumption that would change the outcome. For example, if a market growth rate of 5 per cent is a key assumption, what lower growth rate would have to occur before a substantially different management decision would be taken? For a capital project, this would be the point at which the project would cease to be economical.

Form E in Part IIB (p. 83) can be used to present the Contingency Plan.

*Operating result and financial ratios.* Form F is provided only as an example, for clearly all organizations will have their own formats. However, the following information should be included:

- Net invoicing.
- Gross margin.
- Adjustments.
- Marketing costs.
- Administration costs.
- Interest.
- Operating result.
- Return on sales.
- Return on capital.

See Form F in Part IIB (p. 84).

*Key activity planner.* Finally, you should summarize the key activities and indicate their proposed starting and finishing points. This should help you considerably with monitoring the progress of your annual plan.

Form G in Part IIB (p. 84) can be used as a key activity planner.

*Other.* There may be other information you wish to provide, such as visit plans.

# Format for a headquarters consolidated strategic plan

The author is frequently asked how several SBU strategic marketing plans should be consolidated by senior headquarters marketing personnel. A suggested format for this task is provided below.

The headquarters consolidated strategic plan is arranged under the following headings:

- Directional statement (or mission statement).
- Summary of main features of the plan.
- Financial history (past 5 years).
- Major changes and events since the previous plan.
- Major issues by SBU.
- Strategic objectives by SBU and key statistics.
- Financial goals (next 5 years).
- Appendices.

*Directional statement*
*Role contribution.* This should be a brief statement about the company's role or contribution. Usually it will specify a minimum growth rate for turnover and profit, but it could also encapsulate roles such as opportunity-seeking, service, and so on.

*Definition of the business.* This statement should describe the needs that the company is fulfilling, or the benefits that it is providing for its markets: for example, 'the provision of information to business to facilitate credit decision-making'. Usually, at the corporate level, there will be a number of definitions for its SBU.

It is important that these statements are not so broad as to be meaningless, e.g. Communications', which could mean satellites or pens, or too narrow, e.g. 'Drills' which could become obsolete if a better method for making holes is found.

*Distinctive competence.* All companies should have a distinctive competence. It does not have to be unique, but it must be substantial and sustainable. Distinctive competence can reside in integrity, specialist skills, technology, distribution strength, international coverage, reputation, and so on.

*Indications for future direction.* This section should indicate guidelines for future growth. For example, does the company wish to expand internationally, or to acquire new skills and resources? The purpose of this section is to indicate the boundaries for future business activities.

*Summary of main features of the plan*
Draw a portfolio matrix indicating the current and proposed relative position of each of the SBUs. Alternatively, this can appear later in the plan (see 'Strategic objectives by SBU and Key Statistics', p. 58).

Include a few words summarizing growth in turnover, profit, margins, etc.

Draw a graph indicating simply the total long-term plan. At least two lines are necessary – turnover and profit.

*Financial history (past 5 years)*
Include a bar chart showing relevant financial history – at the very least include turnover and profit for the past 5 years.

*Major changes and events since the previous plan*
Describe briefly the major changes and events (such as divesting a subsidiary) that have occurred during the previous year.

*Major issues by SBU*
*Market characteristics.* Here, it is useful to provide a table listing SBUs, alongside relevant market characteristics. See Table II.15.

*Table II.15* Market characteristics and SBUs

|  | SBU 1 | SBU 2 | SBU 3 | SBU 4 |
|---|---|---|---|---|
| Market size |  |  |  |  |
| Market growth |  |  |  |  |
| Competitive intensity |  |  |  |  |
| Relative market share |  |  |  |  |
| Others |  |  |  |  |

*Competitive characteristics.* Now list the Critical Success Factors by SBU and rate each unit against major competitors. See Table II.16.

*Table II.16* SBU1 and CSFs

| CSFs | Our organization | Competitor 1 | Competitor 2 |
|---|---|---|---|
| CSF 1 |  |  |  |
| CSF 2 |  |  |  |
| CSF 3 |  |  |  |
| CSF 4 |  |  |  |
| CSF 5 |  |  |  |

Repeat this for each SBU.

*Key strategic issues.* This is an extremely important section, as its purpose is to list (possibly by SBU) the key issues facing the company. In essence, this involves stating the really major strengths, weaknesses, opportunities and threats, and indicating how they will be either built on or dealt with.

Key Strategic Issues include technology, regulation, competitive moves, institutional changes, and so on.

### Strategic objectives by SBU and key statistics

This is a summary of the objectives of each SBU. It should obviously be tailored to the specific circumstances of each company. However, an example of what might be appropriate is shown in Table II.17.

*Table II.17*   Summary of objectives

| | Objectives | | | | | | Key Statistics | | | | |
| --- | --- | --- | --- | --- | --- | --- | --- | --- | --- | --- | --- |
| | Market share | | Relative market share | | Real growth | | Sales per employee | | Contribution per employee | | etc. |
| | Now | +5 yr | Now | +5 yr | +5 yr | p.a. | Now | +5 yr | Now | +5 yr | |
| SBU 1 | | | | | | | | | | | |
| SBU 2 | | | | | | | | | | | |
| SBU 3 | | | | | | | | | | | |
| SBU 4 | | | | | | | | | | | |
| SBU 5 | | | | | | | | | | | |

Alternatively, or additionally, draw up a Portfolio Matrix indicating the current and proposed relative positions of each of the SBUs.

### Financial goals (next 5 years)

Draw a bar chart (or a number of bar charts) showing the relevant financial goals. At the very least show turnover and profit by SBU for the next 5 years.

### Appendices

Include whatever detailed appendices are appropriate. Try not to rob the total plan of focus by including too much detail.

# The planning timetable

The major steps and timing for the annual round of strategic and operational planning are described in the following pages.

The planning process has two separate stages, interrelated to provide a review point prior to the detailed quantification of plans. Stage One comprises the statement of key and critical objectives for the full 3-year planning period, to be reviewed with the managing director before the more detailed quantification of the tactical 1-year plan in Stage Two by 30 November for subsequent consolidation into the company plans.

*Planning team's 'kick-off' meeting*

At this meeting, which has to be completed by 31 March, the planning team will outline its expectations for the following planning cycle. The purpose of the meeting is to give the planning team the opportunity to explain corporate policy, report progress during the previous planning cycle, and to give a broad indication of what is expected from each SBU during the forthcoming cycle.

The planning team's review will include an appraisal of performance against plan, as well as a variance analysis. The briefing will give guidance under some of the following headings (as appropriate):

*Financial*
- Gross margins.
- Operating profits.
- Debtors.
- Creditors.
- Cash flow.

*Workforce and organization*
- Organization.
- Succession.
- Training.
- Remuneration.

*Marketing*
- Product development.
- Target markets.
- Market segments.
- Volumes.
- Market shares.
- Pricing.
- Promotion.
- Market research.
- Quality control.
- Customer service.

This meeting is an essential preliminary to the mainstream planning activity that SBUs will subsequently engage in. It is the principal means by which the managing director will ensure that plans do not become stale and repetitive due to over-bureaucratization. Marketing creativity will be the keynote of this meeting.

*Top-down and bottom-up planning*

A cornerstone of the marketing planning philosophy is that there should be widespread understanding at all levels in the organization of the key

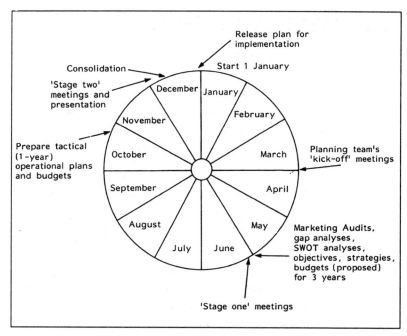

Figure II.15  *Strategic and operational planning cycle*

*Table II.18*  Timetable

| Activity | Deadline |
|---|---|
| Planning team's 'kick-off' meetings with SBU managers to discuss guidelines for the 3-year planning period | 31 March |
| Prepare marketing audits. Do gap analyses. | 30 April |
| Do SWOT analyses, proposed marketing objectives, strategies and budgets (cover full 3-year planning horizon) | 31 May |
| 'Stage One' meetings: presentation to planning team for review | 31 May |
| Prepare short-term (1-year) operational plans and budgets, and SBU managers' final 3-year consolidated marketing plans | 31 October |
| 'Stage Two' meetings: presentation to planning team | 31 November |
| Final consolidation of the marketing plans by head office | 31 December |

objectives that have to be achieved, and of the key means of achieving them. This way, the actions and decisions that are taken by managers will be disciplined by clear objectives that fit together logically as part of a rational purpose. This can only happen if the planning system is firmly based on market-centred analysis that emanates from the SBU itself.

Therefore, after the planning team's 'kick-off' meeting, audits should be carried out by all managers in the SBU down to a level determined by SBU managers. Each manager will also carry out SWOT analyses and set tentative 3-year objectives and strategies, together with proposed budgets for initial consideration by their superior manager. In this way, each superior will be responsible for synthesizing the work of those managers reporting to them.

The major steps in the annual planning cycle are listed in Table II.18 and depicted schematically in Figure II.15.

# PART IIB
# Forms for Action

# The Strategic Marketing Plan

The following forms, when completed, are what you should actually present to your manager or director.

*Form 1*

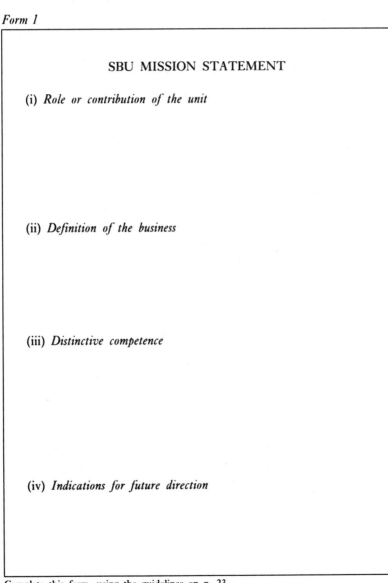

> ## SBU MISSION STATEMENT
>
> (i) *Role or contribution of the unit*
>
>
>
>
>
> (ii) *Definition of the business*
>
>
>
>
>
> (iii) *Distinctive competence*
>
>
>
>
>
> (iv) *Indications for future direction*

Complete this form, using the guidelines on p. 23.

*Form 2*

SUMMARY OF SBU'S PERFORMANCE

|  | Three years ago | Two years ago | Last year | Current year |
|---|---|---|---|---|
| Volume/turnover |  |  |  |  |
| Gross profit $(\frac{margin}{turnover})$ (%) |  |  |  |  |
| Gross margin (turnover – costs) |  |  |  |  |

Summary of reasons for good or bad performances

Complete this form, using the guidelines on pp. 23–4.

So that the figures filled in are meaningful, if possible indicate the rate of inflation of the succeeding 2 years over the base rate (3 years ago).

*Form 3*

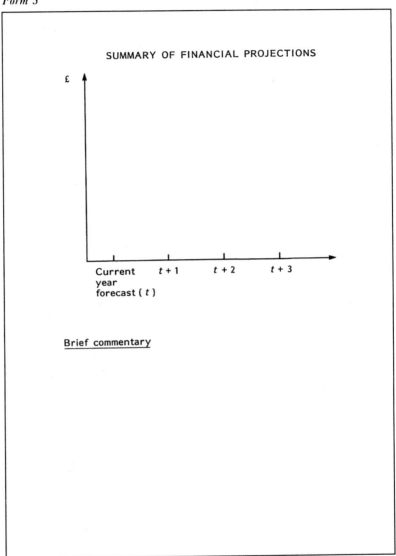

SUMMARY OF FINANCIAL PROJECTIONS

£

Current year forecast ( $t$ )   $t + 1$   $t + 2$   $t + 3$

Brief commentary

Complete this form, using the guidelines on p. 24.

Choose a suitable vertical scale.

Use constant revenue ($t$) so that projections are meaningful: '$t$' means the current year forecast; and 'constant revenue' simply means that you should use the same base year values ($t$) and ignore inflation so that you are comparing like with like.

*Form 4*

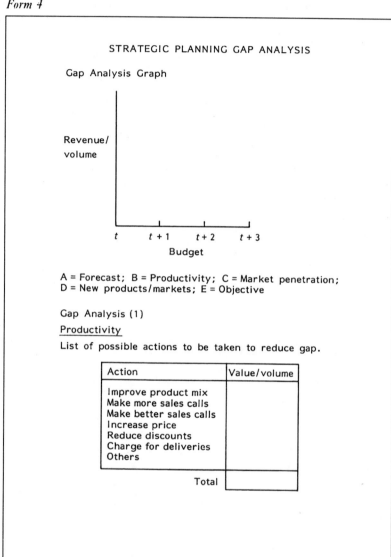

STRATEGIC PLANNING GAP ANALYSIS

Gap Analysis Graph

A = Forecast;  B = Productivity;  C = Market penetration;
D = New products/markets;  E = Objective

Gap Analysis (1)

Productivity

List of possible actions to be taken to reduce gap.

| Action | Value/volume |
|---|---|
| Improve product mix<br>Make more sales calls<br>Make better sales calls<br>Increase price<br>Reduce discounts<br>Charge for deliveries<br>Others | |
| Total | |

Complete this form, using the guidelines on p. 25.
Choose a suitable vertical scale for the Gap Analysis graph.

*Gap analysis (2) – Ansoff product/market matrix (market penetration)*

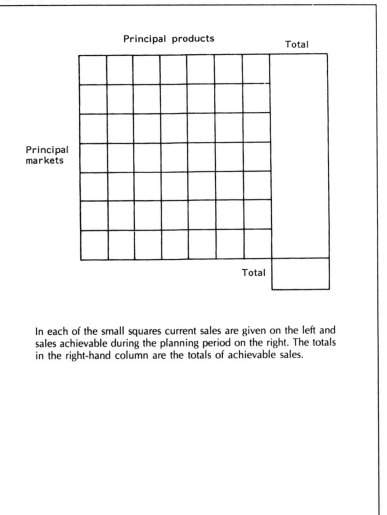

In each of the small squares current sales are given on the left and sales achievable during the planning period on the right. The totals in the right-hand column are the totals of achievable sales.

*Gap analysis (3) – Ansoff product/market matrix (new products, new markets)*

|  | Existing products | New products | Total |

The amounts shown in the small squares represent the values of selling existing products to new markets or new products to existing markets.

*Gap analysis (4)*

| New product | New market | Value |
|---|---|---|
|  |  |  |
|  |  |  |
|  |  |  |
|  |  |  |
|  | Total |  |

This table shows the value of selling new products to new markets.

*Possible ways to change the asset base (if necessary)*

*Form 5*

---

# MARKET OVERVIEW

---

Complete this form using the guidelines on pp. 28–31.

*Form 6 Strategic planning exercise (SWOT analysis)*

FORM 6          STRATEGIC PLANNING EXERCISE (SWOT ANALYSIS)

1   SBU DESCRIPTION      2   CRITICAL SUCCESS FACTORS      3   WEIGHTING

(What business am I in?)

(The few key things that, from the customer's point of view, any competitor has to do right to succeed)

(The importance of each of these CSFs. Scored out of 100)

4   STRENGTHS/WEAKNESSES ANALYSIS

(A score out of 10 is assigned for each CSF for each business and written in the appropriate column. These scores are multiplied by the relevant weighting and the resulting values given in parentheses)

| CSF | Our organisation | Competitor A | Competitor B | Competitor C | Competitor D |
|---|---|---|---|---|---|
| 1 | | | | | |
| 2 | | | | | |
| 3 | | | | | |
| 4 | | | | | |
| 5 | | | | | |
| Total weighted score | | | | | |

5   OPPORTUNITIES/THREATS

(The few key things outside our direct control that have had and will continue to have an impact on the business)

OPPORTUNITIES          THREATS

6   KEY ISSUES THAT NEED TO BE ADDRESSED

7   KEY ASSUMPTIONS FOR THE PLANNING PERIOD      8   KEY OBJECTIVES      9   KEY STRATEGIES

Complete this form, using the guidelines on pp. 31-8.
You should complete one of these forms for each important product/market segment.

*Form 7*

| Competitor Analysis | | | | | | |
|---|---|---|---|---|---|---|
| Main competitor | Market share<br><br>Now    In 3<br>          year's<br>          time | Products/<br>markets | Business<br>direction<br>and<br>current<br>objectives<br>and<br>strategies | Strengths | Weaknesses | Competitive<br>position |
| | | | | | | |

Complete this form, using the guidelines on pp. 36–8.
This form should be completed for each product/market segment under consideration.

*Form 8*

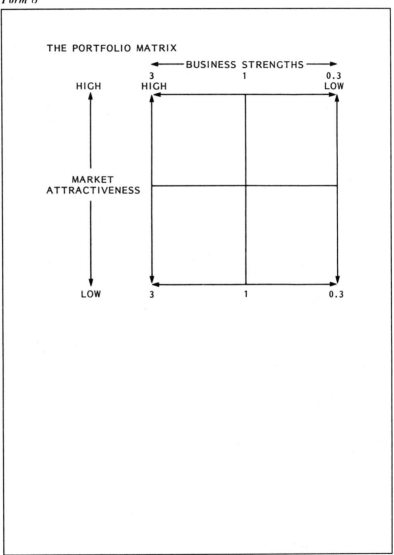

THE PORTFOLIO MATRIX

Complete this form, using the guidelines on pp. 38–46.

*Form 9*

---

# ASSUMPTIONS

---

Complete this form, using the guidelines on p. 46.

## Form 10

DATABASE – I. MARKET SEGMENT SALES VALUES

| Sales values | Last year (t-1) | | | Current year (t) | | | Next year (t + 1) | | | (t + 2) | | | (t+ 3) | | |
|---|---|---|---|---|---|---|---|---|---|---|---|---|---|---|---|
| Key market segments | Total seg- ment | Com- pany sales | Mar- ket share | Total seg- ment | Com- pany sales | Mar- ket share | Total seg- ment | Com- pany sales | Mar- ket share | Total seg- ment | Com- pany sales | Mar- ket share | Total seg- ment | Com- pany sales | Mar- ket share |
| | | | | | | | | | | | | | | | |
| Total | | | | | | | | | | | | | | | |

Complete this form, using the guidelines on pp. 50–1.

## Form 11

DATABASE – II.  MARKET SEGMENT GROSS PROFITS

| Key market segments | Last year (t-1) | | | Current year (t) | | | Next year (t+1) | | | (t + 2) | | | (t + 3) | | |
|---|---|---|---|---|---|---|---|---|---|---|---|---|---|---|---|
| | Sales value | Gross profit | Gross mar- gin (%) | Sales value | Gross profit | Gross mar- gin (%) | Sales value | Gross profit | Gross mar- gin (%) | Sales value | Gross profit | Gross mar- gin (%) | Sales value | Gross profit | Gross mar- gin (%) |
| | | | | | | | | | | | | | | | |
| Total | | | | | | | | | | | | | | | |

Complete this form, using the guidelines on pp. 50–1.

*Form 12*

### DATABASE - III.   PRODUCT GROUP ANALYSIS

| Product groups | Last year (t-1) | | | Current year (t) | | | Next year (t + 1) | | | (t + 2) | | | (t + 3) | | |
|---|---|---|---|---|---|---|---|---|---|---|---|---|---|---|---|
| | Sales value | Gross profit | Gross margin (%) | Sales value | Gross profit | Gross margin (%) | Sales value | Gross profit | Gross margin (%) | Sales value | Gross profit | Gross margin (%) | Sales value | Gross profit | Gross margin (%) |
| | | | | | | | | | | | | | | | |
| Total | | | | | | | | | | | | | | | |

Complete this form, using the guidelines on pp. 50–1.

*Form 13*

SUMMARY OF MAIN MARKETING OBJECTIVES AND
STRATEGIES

Complete this form, using the guidelines on pp. 51–2.

*Form 14*

# FINANCIAL PROJECTIONS FOR 3 YEARS

Complete this form, using the guidelines on p. 52.

# The 1-year operational marketing plan

*Form A*

OBJECTIVES

| Product/ market/ segment/ application/ customer | Volume | | | Value | | | Gross margin | | | Commentary | | |
|---|---|---|---|---|---|---|---|---|---|---|---|---|
| | $t-1$ | $t$ | $t+1$ | $t-1$ | $t$ | $t+1$ | $t-1$ | $t$ | $t+1$ | $t-1$ | $t$ | $t+1$ |
| | | | | | | | | | | | | |
| Comments | | | | | | | | | | | | |

Complete this form, using the guideline on p. 54.

*Form B*

STRATEGIES AND COST

| Strategies | Cost |
|---|---|
| 1 | |
| 2 | |
| 3 | |
| 4 | |
| 5 | |
| 6 | |
| 7 | |
| 8 | |
| 9 | |
| 10 | |
| Comments | |

Complete this form, using the guideline on p. 54.

*Form C*

SUB-OBJECTIVES – ASSESSMENT AND COST

| Product/ market/ segment/ application/ customer | Objective | Strategies | Action | Responsibility | Timing | Cost |
|---|---|---|---|---|---|---|
| | | | | | | |
| | | | | | Total | |

Complete this form, using the guideline on p. 54.

## *Form D*

### SUMMARY OF MARKETING COSTS

|  | $t-1$ | $t$ | $t+1$ | Comments |
|---|---|---|---|---|
| Depreciation |  |  |  |  |
| Salaries |  |  |  |  |
| Postage/telephone/stationery |  |  |  |  |
| Legal and professional |  |  |  |  |
| Training |  |  |  |  |
| Data processing |  |  |  |  |
| Advertising |  |  |  |  |
| Sales promotion |  |  |  |  |
| Travelling and entertainment |  |  |  |  |
| Exhibitions |  |  |  |  |
| Printing |  |  |  |  |
| Meetings/conferences |  |  |  |  |
| Market research |  |  |  |  |
| Internal costs |  |  |  |  |
| Other (specify) |  |  |  |  |
| Total |  |  |  |  |

Complete this form, using the guideline on p. 54.

## *Form E*

### SUGGESTED DOWNSIDE RISK ASSESSMENT FORMAT

| Key assumption | Basis of assumption | What event would have to happen to make this strategy unattractive? | Risk of such an event occurring (probability) | | | Impact if event occurs | Trigger point for action | Actual contingency action proposed |
|---|---|---|---|---|---|---|---|---|
|  |  |  | High $P$ (70–100%) | Medium $P$ (40–69%) | Low $P$ (0–39%) |  |  |  |
|  |  |  |  |  |  |  |  |  |

Complete this form, using the guideline on p. 54.

*Form F*

## OPERATING RESULT AND FINANCIAL RATIOS

|  | $t-1$ | $t$ | $t+1$ |
|---|---|---|---|
| Net invoicing<br>Gross margin<br>Adjustments<br>Marketing costs<br>Administration costs<br>Interest |  |  |  |
| Operating result |  |  |  |
| Other interest and<br>financial costs |  |  |  |
| Result after<br>financial costs |  |  |  |
| Net result |  |  |  |

Complete this form, using the guideline on p. 55.

*Form G*

## KEY ACTIVITY PLANNER

| Activity | Jan. | | | | Feb. | | | | Mar. | | | | Apr. | | | | May | | | | June | | | | July | | | | Aug. | | | | Sept. | | | | Oct. | | | | Nov. | | | | Dec. | | | |
|---|---|---|---|---|---|---|---|---|---|---|---|---|---|---|---|---|---|---|---|---|---|---|---|---|---|---|---|---|---|---|---|---|---|---|---|---|---|---|---|---|---|---|---|---|---|---|---|---|
|  | 1 | 2 | 3 | 4 | 1 | 2 | 3 | 4 | 1 | 2 | 3 | 4 | 1 | 2 | 3 | 4 | 1 | 2 | 3 | 4 | 1 | 2 | 3 | 4 | 1 | 2 | 3 | 4 | 1 | 2 | 3 | 4 | 1 | 2 | 3 | 4 | 1 | 2 | 3 | 4 | 1 | 2 | 3 | 4 | 1 | 2 | 3 | 4 |

Complete this form, using the guideline on p. 55.

# PART III
# Examples of Marketing Plans

It is virtually impossible to find examples of 'model' marketing plans. This is because all organizations are different, and surrounded by varying degrees of complexity and turbulence.

The following marketing plans have been selected, not because they conform perfectly to the prescription provided in this book, but because they illustrate the clarity of purpose that can result from a structured approach to marketing strategy.

Each one can be criticized in several respects, but each one also contains a lot that represents good practice.

# Simon & Jones Ltd

**S**imon & Jones is a small company. Its marketing plan, therefore, has to be a very practical document – certainly a case where an ounce of common sense is worth more than a ton of sophistication.

We believe that this first attempt at producing a 3-year strategic marketing plan is a very creditable effort. What is particularly interesting is how the company thinking conforms to the widely accepted theories about marketing planning. There are many improvements, however, that could be made to this plan, so we make some observations about what these might be.

What follows then are:

1 Some background notes to enable the reader to understand something about the company and its situation. These would not of course appear in a marketing plan.

2 The marketing plan itself.

3 Some observations about the plan to illustrate how marketing planning theory has relevance even for such a small company, and how this plan could be improved.

You will not find Simon & Jones listed in any industry handbook or the *Yellow Pages*. The name, along with some data and other information, has been disguised in order to protect the commercial interests of the real company in its real industrial setting. Nevertheless, this marketing plan sets down all the stages that the company worked through. In that sense it is a very accurate copy of the real thing.

*Background information*
Ken Simon and Barry Jones have worked for most of their lives in the electronics industry. Both are in their early forties and previously worked together for a leading UK company.

Ken Simon's expertise was in the manufacturing side of the business and customer liaison, whereas Barry Jones's was design and quality control. For some years they had planned to leave the relatively safe haven of the large company and start up their own business.

Just under a year ago they made the break and set up Simon & Jones Ltd in a town on the Sussex coast. In addition to themselves, eight people are employed – five test/assembly workers, two administrative staff and a packer-cum-loader-cum-van-driver. Outworkers are also used to complete some of the more simple tasks in their homes.

Ken Simon is the managing director and also responsible for sales. Barry Jones is the technical director responsible for design, quality, buying and in fact most of the day to day activities that are required to keep the company operating.

The business idea behind their move came to them as they struggled to overcome a continual problem that had beset them in their former employment. In essence this was that bought-in components either had too loose a technical specification to meet the sophisticated circuitry requirements required for increasingly demanding end-user applications, or else components of the correct specification were too expensive and uneconomic for volume-manufacturing runs.

While the finger of blame could be pointed at the component manufacturers, they in turn had their problems. For them, the production of 'speciality' items is expensive, because they are predominantly geared up to 'high volume/low cost' manufacturing, where individual batches of components can display a wide variance around their intended performance specification. Alternatives, such as re-engineering and tightening up on the manufacturing specification, or routinely testing every component and discarding those that do not fall within a narrow band, would have the effect of pushing most component costs higher.

Simon and Jones saw a way of exploiting a large component manufacturer's dilemma and converting it into a business opportunity. By buying large batches and accurately characterizing each component, they could produce families of matching products to meet a 'down-line' manufacturer's precise specification. In addition, by arranging these components into frequently used sub-assemblies, they could give this process, of convenience for the manufacturer, added benefits in terms of simplified design, reduced inspection and reduced final assembly costs.

Ken Simon's wealth of contacts in the industry had guaranteed that the new company would get off to a flying start. However, the two directors were surprised at the level of business they generated, and the new options that kept opening up for them in terms of new work in new industries. In the first 8 months the company received approximately £200,000 in sales revenue.

Far from being complacent about these results, Simon and Jones felt that somehow they had to harness their corporate energy and channel it more effectively. Equally, they both harboured secret fears that the 'bubble' could burst, and that the business could dry up just as rapidly as it had developed.

This then was their motivation for producing a strategic marketing plan for the company. What makes their plan so interesting is that the short life of the company meant that there was virtually no historical data to influence their thinking.

*The 3-year strategic marketing plan*

Market review
Analysis of our sales shows that we deal in seven different 'business sectors':

(a) Telecommunications.
(b) Industrial process control.
(c) Fire and security.
(d) Computers.
(e) Medical.
(f) Test equipment.
(g) Military.

To draw any firm conclusions from the sales figures to these business sectors in the short history of the company could be misleading at this stage of our development.

Characteristics of these business sectors
(a) *Telecommunications.* Rapidly growing market with considerable potential from the increasing use of modems. The market is not very price-sensitive and new options could open up if BT's monopoly powers are further reduced.
   The main constraints are the need to conform to BS415 and BTOs long-winded approved procedures.
(b) *Industrial process control.* Expanding market with large demand for special components. Not very price-sensitive, since production tends to be 'low volume/high margin'.
   The main constraint is getting known and achieving a relationship with this sector, especially in the ten or so major companies.
(c) *Fire and security.* Highly competitive, 'high volume/low cost' business with short lead times and short product life-cycles. The main constraints are that the high-volume demand makes it 'interesting' for large component manufacturers to provide 'specials'. Equally, we could be swamped with high-volume work. We don't really know enough about the industry to see what price-insensitive opportunities exist.
(d) *Computers.* Some opportunities, but since most computer production is carried on outside the UK, the long-term prospects do not look particularly attractive.
(e) *Medical.* Like computers, much of the medical market is dominated by overseas companies, mainly Japanese. This, coupled with the uncertainties surrounding public-sector spending, make this sector questionable.

(f) *Test equipment.* Market is dominated by foreign competition, and the low volume to be expected from UK manufacturers doesn't make this an attractive sector.

(g) *Military.* Potentially lucrative market once we qualify as an approved supplier.

The main constraints are the stringent (therefore expensive) quality-control procedures, the long lead times and relatively low-volume orders.

The attractiveness of the above business sectors is shown in Table III.1.

*Table III.1*    Industrial sector attractiveness

| Attractiveness criteria | Industrial sectors | | | | | | |
|---|---|---|---|---|---|---|---|
| | Telecoms | Ind. proc. control | Fire and security | Military | Computer | Medical | Test equipment |
| Growth potential | 7 | 7 | 7 | 6 | 3 | 3 | 3 |
| Market size (UK) | 8 | 7 | 8 | 6 | 4 | 2 | 2 |
| Profitability | 8 | 8 | 5 | 10 | 7 | 7 | 5 |
| Lack of 'competition' | 6 | 7 | 6 | 7 | 6 | 8 | 6 |
| 'Reachability' | 9 | 10 | 5 | 2 | 2 | 2 | 2 |
| Use our products | 8 | 7 | 8 | 3 | 3 | 4 | 4 |
| Total | 46 | 46 | 39 | 34 | 25 | 26 | 22 |

Key = 10 points for highly attractive → 1 point for minimally attractive

Table III.2 shows the conclusions to be drawn from Table III.1.

*Table III.2*    Relative attractiveness of different business sectors

| High | Medium | Low |
|---|---|---|
| Industrial process Control Telecommunications | Fire and security Military | Computers Medical Test equipment |

## Competition and competitors

(a) All competitors are large companies, some are even multi-nationals, and all are component manufacturers.

(b) Of the nine companies we consider to be our main competitors, (i) three do not produce 'specials'; (ii) six will only produce them in large runs; and (iii) none will tackle small runs of 'tailor-made' components.

(c) No competitor routinely provides the full range of components supplied by us.
(d) None provide the same type of technical support as we do.
(e) No competitor has the flexibility that we have to respond quickly to changes in customer requirements.
(f) Two competitors have a bad reputation for prices being too high.
(g) Two others have a poor image in the market.
(h) Three are considered to have an inadequate product range.

By placing ourselves between the mass production component manufacturers and the fabricators of electronic goods and adding value (in customers' terms) to everything we handle, we have no direct competitors.

In the short term this type of specialization gives us a competitive advantage, but it might also encourage new entrants into this field or cause the large companies to reconsider their marketing strategies. We shall have to monitor these possible changes and not get too complacent.

Features and benefits
The features that we believe make Simon & Jones different from competitors, and how they translate into customer benefits, are shown in Table III.3.

*Table III.3* Advantages possessed by Simon & Jones

| Features | Benefits |
| --- | --- |
| 100% conformance to spec. guaranteed | Reduced sampling to labour costs. No scrap or re-work – reduced labour and materials cost |
| Complete applications engineering service | Cheaper, more practical solutions to engineering problems. Cheaper manufactured products |
| Single 'component' instead of many parts | Reduced assembly costs. Lower stock-holdings costs |
| Price is competitive with any alternative solution to the problem | Cheaper material costs |
| Low volumes, short runs and flexible scheduling | Convenience, lower stock holdings, compatible with JIT schedules |
| Improved appearance of the product | Better marketability |
| Good reputation and reliable performance | Customer confidence, predictability and better scheduling |

Product review
(a) The main product range consists of:
  (i) LED (Light Emitting Diode) assemblies.
  (ii) IR (infra-red) switches.
  (iii) Detectors.
  (iv) Emitters.
  (v) Couplers/decouplers.

(b) Our services are:

  (vi) Cropping and forming.
  (vii) Lead additions and soldering.

The customer benefits these products and services provide are shown in Table III.4.

Table III.4    Customer benefits

| Products and services | Major benefits score 1–10 pts Product (i) | (ii) | Medium benefits score 1–6 pts Product (iii) | (iv) | (v) | Lesser benefits score 1–3 pts Service (vi) | (vii) | Total score | Rank order |
|---|---|---|---|---|---|---|---|---|---|
| (i) LED Assys | 7 | 8 | 4 | 5 | 6 | 3 | 2 | 35 | 3 |
| (ii) IR switches | 8 | 4 | 5 | 4 | 5 | 2 | 3 | 31 | 7 |
| (iii) Detectors | 9 | 10 | 6 | 4 | 4 | 1 | 3 | 37 | 1 |
| (iv) Emitters | 9 | 10 | 6 | 4 | 4 | 1 | 3 | 37 | 1 |
| (v) Couplers/ decouplers | 8 | 8 | 6 | 4 | 5 | 1 | 3 | 35 | 3 |
| (vi) Cropping and forming | 5 | 8 | 6 | 6 | 2 | 2 | 3 | 32 | 6 |
| (vii) Leads & soldering | 6 | 7 | 6 | 6 | 3 | 3 | 3 | 34 | 5 |

Benefit range is illustrated in Table III.5.

Table III.5    Benefit range

| Major benefits | Medium benefits | Lesser benefits |
|---|---|---|
| 1 Guaranteed conformance 2 Complete application engineering service | 3 Single component instead of many 4 Price is competitive 5 Low-volume, short-run, flexible scheduling | 6 Improved appearance 7 Good reputation and reliable performance |

Use of products and services by industrial sector
See Table III.6.

*Table III.6*  Products and services per industrial sector

| Products | T' COMM | PROC. CON-TROL | FIRE & SEC. | COMP. SEC. | MED. | TEST | MILITARY EQUIP. |
|---|---|---|---|---|---|---|---|
| **Industrial sector** | | | | | | | |
| LED assemblies | ✓ | ✓ | ✓ | ✓ | ✓ | x | x |
| IR switches | ✓ | ✓ | ✓ | ✓ | ·✓ | x | ✓ |
| Detectors | ✓ | x | ✓ | x | ✓ | x | ✓ |
| Emitters | ✓ | x | ✓ | x | ✓ | x | ✓ |
| Couplers/decouplers | ✓ | ✓ | ✓ | ✓ | ✓ | ✓ | ✓ |
| **Services** | | | | | | | |
| Cropping and forming | ✓ | ✓ | ✓ | ✓ | ✓ | ✓ | ✓ |
| Leads and soldering | x | ✓ | x | x | x | ✓ | x |
| Applications score | 6 | 5 | 6 | 4 | 6 | 3 | 5 |
| Importance of benefits | | | | | | | |
| Guaranteed conformance | 10 | 6 | 3 | 9 | 7 | 5 | 10 |
| Complete application service | 2 | 7 | 7 | 4 | 4 | 7 | 4 |
| Single component | 6 | 5 | 4 | 4 | 4 | 4 | 3 |
| Price is competitive | 3 | 4 | 6 | 3 | 4 | 3 | 3 |
| Low volume, short run | 2 | 4 | 5 | 4 | 2 | 4 | 4 |
| Improved appearance | 3 | 3 | 1 | 2 | 3 | 3 | 3 |
| Good reputation | 3 | 3 | 3 | 3 | 3 | 2 | 3 |
| Benefits total | 29 | 32 | 28 | 29 | 27 | 28 | 30 |
| Sector Attractiveness (applications + benefits) | 35 | 37 | 34 | 33 | 33 | 31 | 35 |

KEY

✓ = product used in industry sector

x = product not used

Applications score = no. of ✓s

Major benefits scored 1–10 pts

Medium benefits scored 1–6 pts

Lesser benefits scored 1–3 pts

The analysis in Table III.6 confirms our earlier assessment about markets/industrial sectors. The military sector could be more attractive than we originally thought. We should give it more attention as a potential growth area.

Product life-cycles
As there is little historical data to plot life-cycles, estimates have been based upon what authoritative sources have said about the technological developments in our various fields, i.e. our products will become redundant as and when newer technology becomes available. However, the chances are that even with new technologies we will be able to continue to operate in a similar way, but offering a new generation of components. See Table III.7.

Our existing product/service range would appear to provide us with a stable base for the business over the next few years. As we collect more data, we will monitor life-cycles more accurately.

Pricing review
Most products are made to order against a price that has been negotiated with the customer.

*Table III.7*    Life cycles of products and services

| Products and services | Life-cycles |
|---|---|
| LED assemblies | Possible replacement by CRT (Cathode Ray Tubes) as they become miniaturised, but only in some applications. Reasonable to expect at least 10 years' life |
| IR switches | Becoming increasingly popular for replacing mechanical and magnetic switches. More applications are likely to be found. Again, at least 10 years' life can be expected |
| Detectors and emitters | No substitute on the horizon, increased demand expected over next 10 years |
| Couplers/ decouplers | This function could be built into integrated circuits as chip technology develops. Life of perhaps 4–5 years |
| Cropping and forming | Not tied so directly to technology but is likely to be continued for next 2–3 years |
| Leads and soldering | Only relevant in process control sector. We will probably reduce this service and use the labour more productively elsewhere |

Our policy of accurately costing each product and then adding a 40 per cent margin as the minimum price seems to work well. The fact we treat this figure as the 'go/no go' criterion provides us with a good safeguard.

For our time in business the average net margin has worked out at 48 per cent.

At present there is no need for a more complex pricing policy. The fact that our products are unobtainable elsewhere justifies our high margin policy. As the company grows, or if we decide to target specific markets seriously, our pricing policy might need to be reviewed.

Promotion review

The key factor in the sales process is getting the design engineer of the manufacturer to realise that (i) he has a problem; and (ii) we can solve it for him cost-effectively. Establishing contact with design engineers and then developing good working relations with them are essential for success.

To date three types of promotional activity other than face-to-face meetings have been used. See Table III.8.

Most sales have been generated by the managing director networking among his contacts throughout the electronics industry. However, while personal visits have been productive they have also been very time-consuming.

Exhibitions look to be a fruitful source of leads, but we will have to be more structured in the way we tackle them. We needed printed

*Table III.8*    Promotional activity

| Activity | Objective | Expenditure (£s) |
|---|---|---|
| Exhibitions | To inform, persuade and interest new customers | 4,250 |
| Catalogues | To inform engineers, designers and buyers —sent by mail shot | 3,780 |
| Advertising in trade journals and catalogues | To inform and create awareness among designers and engineers. To improve our image as a supplier | 2,023 |
| | Total | 10,053 |

materials, and so the investment in catalogues was probably justified. Whether or not the advertising in journals is working for us is open to question, but it isn't that expensive.

The big question is 'Can we afford the luxury of the MD being on the road nearly all the time?' The other question is 'Who could do the selling job better?'

The way we have tackled promotion to date has been somewhat arbitrary but nevertheless reasonably successful. However, if our investment is going to pay off, we need to have some clear rationale behind our action plan and find better methods of targeting our promotional expenditure.

Distribution

It is our policy to work closely with each customer and deliver direct. There seems to be no reason to change this. However, our focus has been strictly limited to the UK. It therefore could be worthwhile to explore some form of reciprocal trading arrangement with a mainland European company whereby:

(a) They sell some of our more standard products.
(b) We add some of their products to our range.

This is something that will have to be investigated over the next year. A company similar in size to our own would be ideal.

SWOT analysis

The analysis of our strengths, weaknesses, opportunities and threats worked out as shown in Table III.9.

*Table III.9*    SWOT analysis

| Strengths | Weaknesses |
|---|---|
| • Expertise – products and technology.<br>• Flexibility – fast response.<br>• No competitors – in the direct sense.<br>• High performance – quality and delivery.<br>• Product range – long life-cycles.<br>• Growing markets – esp. telecom and process control.<br>• Spread – not tied to a single industry. | • Dependence on major component suppliers not being able to tighten specs or produce 'specials'.<br>• Sales dependent on MD.<br>• Small product range.<br>• Advertising not thought out.<br>• Size of labour force is a limit to throughput.<br>• Only trade in UK. |
| Opportunities | Threats |
| • Increased penetration in telecom, process control, military and fire and security.<br>• Expand product range and European market through co-operation with mainland company.<br>• Focus business effort on key pay-off areas.<br>• Become an 'agent' for a large components manufacturer.<br>• Build on experience and develop consultancies with large manufacturers. | • Component manufacturers tighten up their tolerances.<br>• Look-alike small businesses start up as competition.<br>• There is a further decline in UK manufacturing if current interest rates continue at such high levels.<br>• Preferred business sectors switch their manufacturing to Far East or a developing country. |

## Assumptions

Some assumptions have been made as this analysis progressed. They are:

1 *The market needs our products and services.* From our limited time in business this assumption appears to hold true. Technology will not change so quickly that we are left 'high and dry'.

2 *No new competitor will start up in the next year.* The combination of our expertise and relationship with customers would make it difficult for a newcomer to make any inroads into our business in the short term. So while it is in theory possible for a competitor to start up, from the planning point of view there is a high level of confidence to accept the above assumption.

3 *Component suppliers will not increase their prices dramatically.* If they did, it might affect our ability to add a 40–50 per cent margin on the cost of products. There is no evidence that large price increases are in the pipe-line.

4 *The managing director remains in good health.* If the MD was unable to run the business due to ill-health, there could be far-reaching implications for the company. Confidence that he is fit and healthy is high, but the risks of an accident are clearly unknown.

Marketing objectives and strategies
Objectives and strategies have been worked out, and they appear in Table
III.10.

*Table III.10*  Marketing objectives and strategies

| Objectives | Markets | Strategies |
|---|---|---|
| Increase market penetration and level of business | Telecoms Industrial process control | a) Increase level of personal visits to new customers and influence more people in DMUs<br>b) Maintain prices at current levels (reduce only if competition starts up)<br>c) Aim for targets on sales plan<br>d) Develop new products/services either i) through customer contact ii) through agreement with mainland European Co. to sell their products<br>e) Improve communications |
| Abandon | Medical Computers Test equipment | a) No promotional effort<br>b) Quote high prices to discourage all but the most lucrative business<br>c) Low sales targets |
| Increase level of business | Fire and security | a) Improved communications<br>b) Maintain prices<br>c) Extend sales through the range to existing customers<br>d) Sales visits at same level |
| Maintain level of business (as proportion of total sales) | Military | a) Get approval as contractor<br>b) Establish a reputation<br>c) Assess the potential of this market<br>d) Maintain prices<br>e) Targets as per sales plan |

Sales plan
In order to achieve the sales plan (Table III.11), the managing director
will have to spend more time with actual and potential customers. A

*Table III.11*  Sales plan

| Business sector | Current year Value (£) | % | Year 1 Value (£) | % | Year 2 Value (£) | % | Year 3 Value (£) | % |
|---|---|---|---|---|---|---|---|---|
| Telecoms | 60,450 | 31 | 82,500 | 33 | 112,000 | 35 | 151,200 | 36 |
| Industrial proc. control | 54,600 | 28 | 75,000 | 30 | 102,400 | 32 | 138,600 | 33 |
| Fire and security | 35,100 | 18 | 47,500 | 19 | 64,000 | 20 | 88,200 | 21 |
| Military | 19,500 | 10 | 25,000 | 10 | 32,000 | 10 | 42,000 | 10 |
| Computers | 9,750 | 5 | 7,500 | 3 | 3,200 | 1 | ...... | 0 |
| Medical | 9,750 | 5 | 7,500 | 3 | 3,200 | 1 | ...... | 0 |
| Test equipment | 5,850 | 3 | 5,000 | 2 | 3,200 | 1 | ...... | 0 |
|  | 195,000 | 100 | 250,000 | 100 | 320,000 | 100 | 420,000 | 100 |

new salesman would not have the same range of experience as the MD, nor the confidence of his contacts.

Therefore the technical director will assume some of the MD's duties and an administration manager/sales office manager will be recruited.

Communications plan
The communications *objectives* will be the following:

1 To inform the buying/decision-making community about the benefits to be derived from our product range.
2 To communicate our strengths and build customer confidence.
3 To generate enquiries.

The *target audience* will be:

1 Design engineers.
2 Project engineers.
3 Buyers.
4 Other occasional participants in the buying process.

In all we estimate that there will only be 1,000–1,500 key people to influence, and so mass media will be inappropriate.

To achieve objectives 1 and 2 above use will be made of catalogues, direct mail, and a newsletter (format to be decided). To achieve objectives 2 and 3 above we will use exhibitions.

The budget allocation will be as shown in Table III.12. The proportional spend remains approximately 5 per cent of sales revenue.

*Table III.12*    Budget for communications

| Current year | Year 1 | Year 2 | Year 3 |
|---|---|---|---|
| £10,053 | £12,500 | £16,000 | £21,000 |

*Observations on the marketing plan*
Marketing planning sequence
The generally accepted marketing planning process is shown in Figure III.1. Simon & Jones comes very close to following this pattern. Its corporate objectives are presumably to get sales revenue doubled over the next 3 years and to maintain its competitor free niche for as long as possible.

Not much attention seems to have been given to considering alternative strategies, but the firm's initial strategy when starting the business

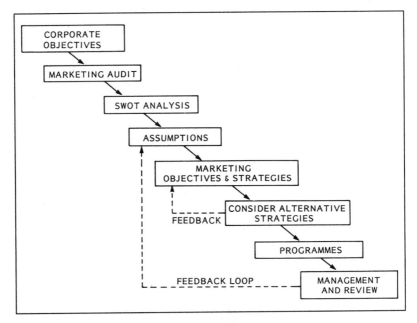

Figure III.1 *Marketing planning process*

seems to have been working quite well. Fine-tuning and clearer focusing could be all that is required.

The treatment of each stage in the planning process has been tackled in a fairly pragmatic way, certainly at a level of sophistication in keeping with the company. The general lack of data has been handled quite well. The use of informed opinion, educated guesses and weighted subjective analysis demonstrates that the company is taking its future seriously.

Portfolio matrix

Had the company been aware of the Portfolio Matrix theory, it could have constructed Figure III.2 from the information provided in the sections on 'Sector attractiveness' and 'Benefit analysis'.

The data are reproduced in Table III.13.

Table III.13  Data for portfolio matrix

| | Industrial sector | Tele-com | Industrial process control | Fire and security | Military | Computer | Medical | Test equip-ment |
|---|---|---|---|---|---|---|---|---|
| A | 46 | 46 | 39 | 34 | 25 | 26 | 22 |
| B (s) | 29 | 32 | 28 | 30 | 29 | 27 | 28 |

A = Attractiveness
B (s) = Benefits (strengths)

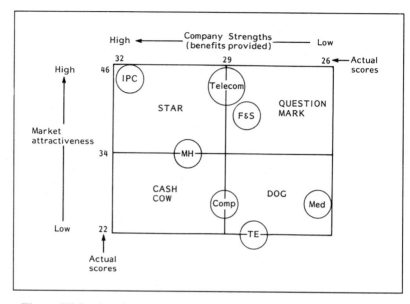

Figure III.2    *Portfolio matrix. Cross axes drawn at mid-points of score distributions*

With this information the company strategy, while being roughly along the right lines, could be usefully modified thus:

1 More effort to develop business strengths in 'Telecommunications' and 'Fire and security' sectors.
2 Major part of the promotions budget should be spent on above two sectors, plus 'Industrial process control'.
3 'Military' sector could be 'milked' for even higher profit margins.
4 'Computers' might not be discarded quite so readily but treated as a 'cash dog' in the short term.

The decision to withdraw from 'Medical' and 'Test equipment' is clearly vindicated.

Ansoff matrix
While the marketing objectives were not presented in diagrammatic form, they do in fact fit neatly on the product/market matrix. See Figure III.3.

What Figure III.3 illustrates is that the company's strengths are essentially product-based rather than market-based. Equally, in a start-up position, it is probably a sensible stance to consolidate the business in existing markets before expending energy seeking out new ones. For

| | Products | |
|---|---|---|
| | Existing | New |
| **Existing**<br><br>**Markets**<br><br>**New** | Telecoms<br>Ind. proc. control<br>(increase sales)<br>Military (maintain)<br>Computers ⎤ abandon<br>Medical ⎬ by pricing<br>Test equip. ⎦ high | Telecom and IPC<br>(develop new products<br>either with customers<br>or through co-operative<br>agreement with<br>European partner) |
| | Fire and security<br>(find price-insensitive<br>parts of the market<br>and sell through range)<br><br>Potential sales through<br>European partner | No plans for<br>diversification |

Figure III.3    *Product/market matrix*

Simon & Jones it would appear to be easier to develop new products than new markets.

Possibility of new entrants as competitors
While the company claim that this is low, it would clearly be a damaging prospect if it should happen. In fact the company situation is a good illustration of the work of Porter on competitive forces. See Figure III.4.

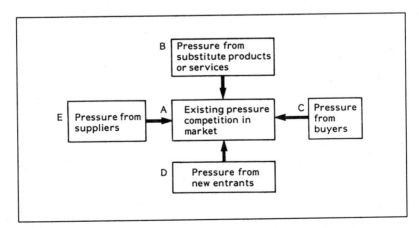

Figure III.4    *Pressure distribution re competitive forces*

Looking at Simon & Jones's situation in the context of Figure III.4 the following observations could be made.

1 *Inter-firm competition.* There is no direct competition except at the periphery of the business.
2 *Substitutes.* There are few substitutes at present, and the position will remain that way unless technology changes.
3 *Buyers.* Large-order buyers could exert pressure on the company, but while it maintains a unique product range for essentially 'low volume/high margin' applications, the buyer's power is marginalized.
4 *New entrants.* Barriers to entry are expertise and knowledge of the customer's industry. Simon & Jones, being first into the market, are moving along a 'learning curve' with every day that passes. This experience is likely to retain the company's market dominance in the foreseeable future, even if a new entrant appears.
5 *Suppliers.* Suppliers have high power. If they changed their manufacturing policies about producing specials, then Simon & Jones could be threatened. However, as a small company, Simon & Jones would always have an advantage regarding reduced overheads and greater flexibility.

One strategy that could minimize the threat from a supplier, and at the same time guarantee continued supplies, would be for the company to enter an arrangement whereby it became the 'bespoke tailoring' unit of one of the manufacturers.

# Wilcox & Simmonds Project Management Ltd

*Introduction*

Wilcox & Simmonds has a long, and on the whole, distinguished record of supplying the UK construction industry with a range of specialist goods and services. The Project Management Division was recently set up to run as an autonomous unit to provide project management services to the construction industry, something that is a relatively new idea in this business sector.

Project management originally developed in the heavy, civil and process engineering industries. It takes responsibility for the planning, control and coordination of a project from inception to completion, with the objective of meeting the client's requirements of achieving completion on time, within the target cost and to the required quality standards.

During a construction project a whole range of functional specialists might be used – say architects, structural engineers, service engineers, quantity surveyors and building contractors. Very large projects might also include town planners and civil engineers. The project manager's task can be to recommend people to fulfil these roles, or to work with those of the client's choice. Essentially the project manager becomes the 'hub' of a network of interrelated activities, the output of which is dictated by his budgetary planning skills and his ability to influence and cajole everyone to deliver their particular contribution at the required time.

The key benefit for the client is that all progress can be monitored through one person, and if things are going wrong, there is again only one person to deal with. Although a client company might have a department capable in theory of tackling such work, in practice there is often not the required wide range of expertise and experience to sustain the project management role.

Thus the UK construction industry, with its tradition of separating design from construction, and its propensity for developing managers as functional specialists, appeared to be a suitable candidate for a project management approach. It was this opportunity that spurred the company to set up its new division.

So new is project management in the building industry that its role is not yet fully accepted, nor is there an established pricing structure.

It is against this background that the Chief Executive and his team prepare for the next 3 years, after an eventful and quite successful first year in business. What follows is the business plan produced by the Project Management Division.

In order to protect confidentiality, all names, locations and values have been changed. However, the integrity of the company's planning process still remains to provide an interesting example of business planning, from which we can all learn.

*Review of first full year's trading*

Although financial targets were met, a substantial amount of time was devoted to setting up and staffing our three offices. In addition, it was difficult to recruit staff experienced in both project management and the construction industry; therefore a considerable amount of training had to be provided.

However, we now have an administrative base, the personnel and technical procedures. This means that project managers can start to focus on building up the business in a planned and sustained way, rather than chasing work as and when opportunities present themselves. See Tables III.14, III.15 and III.16.

*Table III.14* Financial position

|  | Budget (£000s) | Actual (£000s) |
|---|---|---|
| Income | 2,352 | 2,573 |
| Expenditure | 1,970 | 2,052 |
| Profit | 382 | 521 |

*Table III.15* Personnel

|  | Actual | Deviation from plan |
|---|---|---|
|  |  | Professional staff |
| Croydon | 13 | −3 |
| Coventry | 14 | 0 |
| Manchester | 5 | 0 |
|  | Actual | Deviation from plan |
|  |  | Administrative staff |
| Croydon | 7 | +1 |
| Coventry | 5 | −1 |
| Manchester | 1 | 0 |
| TOTAL | 45 |  |

*Table III.16* Analysis of profit

|  | Turnover | Profit |
|---|---|---|
| Project management | £1,750,000 | £250,000 |
| Construction management | £860,000 | £271,000 |
| TOTAL |  | £521,000 |

*Market overview*

Competition
There are probably at most only about forty companies set up to offer
a similar service to ours. Of these companies, we are one of the largest,
in terms of project managers employed. However, there are a number
of other types of competitors who partially compete with us by offering a reduced range of services. These companies fall into the broad
categories shown in Table III.17.

*Table III.17* Companies in PM field

| Organization category | Services |
| --- | --- |
| 1 *Management consultants* These are often parts of major accounting firms. | Specialist advice feasibility studies. |
| 2 *Management contractors* Usually parts of large building contractors. | Management of site work, but little involvement in design. |
| 3 *Civil engineering contractors* (with project management depts). | Tend to stay in civil engineering. Also undertake feasibility studies. |
| 4 *Quantity surveyors with PM depts* | Tend to limit their role to providing information at meetings, etc. Some duplicate the work of building contractors. |
| 5 *PM depts of client companies.* | Do not have the expertise to compete with us on quality. |

Market trends
The construction industry is a very large, if fragmented, market. Over
the last 10 years it has grown steadily at a rate of approximately 5.5
per cent per annum. The project management market we estimate to
have a potential value of £120m. Our current market share of this is
2.1 per cent.
    However, we believe there will be a rapid increase in sales of project
management for a number of reasons:

● More clients will perceive the need for it as it becomes increasingly
  accepted in the industry.
● Clients seek new solutions to improve their performance.
● The rate of change in building technology makes project management
  ever more complex and difficult for those not trained in it (the major-
  ity of construction managers).
● Architects are failing to fulfil clients' needs in terms of providing
  value-for-money solutions.
● There is increasing pressure to shorten the inception to completion
  time span.

Market structure
There are two driving forces for the construction industry:

1 Property developers and investors who create facilities for sale or lease. Included in this category are insurance companies, banks, pension funds, investment companies.
2 Property occupiers who create facilities for their own use. In this category are firms from the private sector, such as manufacturing, retailing, distribution and leisure. There is also a sizeable public sector, which includes government ministries, local authorities, public utilities, public transport and health authorities.

Strategic business units
It would make sense to manage our business through five specific business units:

1 *Regional project management.* Managing medium to large projects (ideally over £250,000 construction turnover per month) in all principal markets.
2 *Construction management.* Managing fast track, complex projects (ideally over £1m construction turnover per month) which require a site-based construction team. This SBU would focus on commercial owner occupier/developers in the South East.
3 *Special projects.* A design and management service to small building projects, operating mainly in the developer, pension fund, owner–occupier markets.
4 *Manufacturing process projects.* Managing manufacturing plants, machinery installations and associated commercial buildings. The principal markets will be industrial and warehousing.
5 *Major projects.* Projects which require a dedicated team and are likely to be in the order of £2m construction turnover per month. The initial market to be targeted will be investor/developer, although this unit will operate in all principal markets.

SBUs 4 and 5 will not come on stream for another year.

Mission statement
Our review of our first year has not caused us to be swayed from our original statement of intent: *To become the leading company supplying project management within the construction industry.*
We will achieve this by:

● Establishing a reputation for quality and successful completions.
● Having the largest market share.

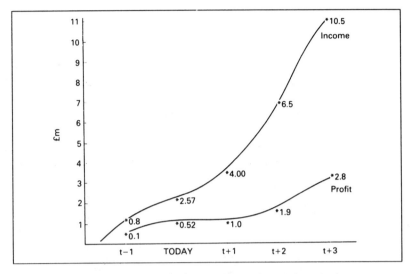

Figure III.5 *Project management – financial projections*

- Being the first choice of clients seeking project management.
- Being the first choice of the best candidates in the job market.

Above all we must be clear about what we are striving to achieve at a time when there are many potential opportunities in the market place.

We believe a key to success is to break our organisation into strategic business units.

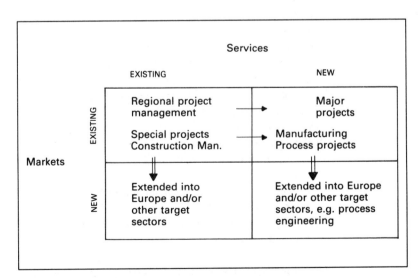

Figure III.6   *Ansoff matrix*

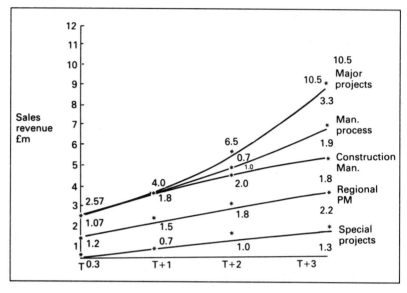

Figure III.7    *Gap analysis*

Financial projections
Financial projections are illustrated in Figure III.5.

Ansoff Matrix
This matrix is illustrated in Figure III.6.

Gap analysis
Gap analysis is illustrated in Figure III.7.

*SWOT analysis*
The analysis in Table III.18 holds true for all the SBUs.

*Critical success factors*
Regional project management
Issues to be addressed include the following requirements:

1 To improve professionalism and motivation of staff, by training and better field management.
2 To improve service surround to provide better value for money. (See also Table III.19.)

Construction management
Issues to be addressed include the following requirements:

*Table III.18* SWOT analysis

| Strengths | Weaknesses |
|---|---|
| • Reputation of W & S in the construction industry in general.<br>• Regional representation in growth areas of UK economy.<br>• High expertise in PM of staff.<br>• One of the largest companies.<br>• Now have a business plan.<br>• Wealth of contacts in the industry via W & S.<br>• Starting with a 'clean sheet' and can get it right, from the start. | • Training of new staff needs to be improved, both in quality and duration (too long).<br>• Lack of detailed market information.<br>• Need more/better promotional material.<br>• We have made mistakes in recruiting PMs. Some do not fit our 'culture'. More attention to selection and better employment package required.<br>• PMs are excellent individuals but do not yet function well in teams.<br>• To date we have been chasing any work just to meet targets and have not been focused.<br>• Technical procedures still need to be improved.<br>• Need to establish unique selling points/selling skills. |
| **Opportunities** | **Threats** |
| • PM is in its infancy in the construction industry.<br>• Large potential market.<br>• Expand by acquisition if necessary.<br>• Joint ventures, in UK and Europe.<br>• Traditional structure of construction industry lends itself to PM.<br>• Few serious competitors at present. | • Interest rates increase even more, and trigger off a recession.<br>• Entry of new competitors.<br>• Large contractors develop their own PM depts.<br>• Inability to recruit sufficiently high-calibre staff to sustain growth.<br>• PM does not really 'catch on' in the construction industry. |

*Table III.19* Regional project management

| CSF | Weighting | Score v. competition | Total |
|---|---|---|---|
| 1 Staff are perceived by clients as highly professional | 3 | 5 | 15 |
| 2 We provide value for money | 2 | 6 | 12 |
| 3 Our corporate reputation and track record | 2 | 8 | 16 |
| 4 Staff are motivated to win business | 3 | 5 | 18 |
| | 10 | out of 10 | 58/100 |

1 To improve consultant teamwork.
2 To look for ways to offer more value for money. (See also Table III.20.)

Table III.20 Construction management

| CSF | Weighting | Score v. competition | Total |
|---|---|---|---|
| 1 Early identification of opportunity | 3 | 7 | 21 |
| 2 Demonstrate knowledge of client's business | 2 | 8 | 16 |
| 3 High level of consultant teamwork | 2 | 4 | 8 |
| 4 Value for money | 2 | 6 | 12 |
| 5 Track record | 1 | 7 | 7 |
| | 10 | out of 10 | 64/100 |

Table III.21 Special projects

| CSF | Weighting | Score v. competition | Total |
|---|---|---|---|
| 1 Close contact with clients | 1 | 6 | 6 |
| 2 Demonstration of early success | 3 | 6 | 18 |
| 3 Flexibility to adapt to changing client needs | 3 | 8 | 24 |
| 4 Value for money | 2 | 8 | 16 |
| 5 Track record | 1 | 6 | 6 |
| | 10 | out of 10 | 70/100 |

Special projects
Issues to be addressed include the following requirements:

1 To improve contact with clients – establish schedules.
2 To improve and publicize track record.
3 To reappraise staffing levels at front end of projects in order to develop more momentum and hence quicker results.

Manufacturing process projects
Issues to be addressed include the following requirements:

1 To improve intelligence sources.
2 To develop more expertise about client business through recruiting people with different appropriate career backgrounds *or* buy out a suitable company to gain right expertise.

Major projects
Issues to be addressed include the following requirements:

1 To improve market intelligence.
2 To develop teamwork.
3 To look for ways of demonstrating quick paybacks to client.

*Table III.22* Manufacturing process projects

| CSF | Weighting | Score v. competition | Total |
|---|---|---|---|
| 1 Early identification of opportunity | 3 | 5 | 15 |
| 2 Can talk clients' language | 4 | 5 | 20 |
| 3 Value for money | 2 | 8 | 16 |
| 4 Track record | 1 | 7 | 7 |
| | 10 | out of 10 | 58/100 |

*Table III.23* Major projects

| CSF | Weighting | Score v. competition | Total |
|---|---|---|---|
| 1 Dedicated team of high quality. | 3 | 6 | 18 |
| 2 Value for money. | 2 | 7 | 14 |
| 3 Swift evidence of impact of services. | 2 | 7 | 14 |
| 4 Early identification of opportunity. | 3 | 3 | 15 |
| | 10 | out of 10 | 61/100 |

*Assumptions*

Underlying all of the foregoing analyses were the following assumptions.

1 The growth rate of the construction industry will continue at its average rate of the last few years = 1 per cent.
2 Interest rates will not go any higher.
3 Investor confidence stays reasonably buoyant in the short and medium term.
4 There is a continuing growth in the demand for project management.
5 A change of government (should it happen) will not lead to a significant change in the economic prospects of the construction industry.

*Portfolio analysis*

Within regional project management it was possible to break down the current and potential business in terms of our competence in dealing with key market segments and their attractiveness. The results are shown in Figure III.8. It is intended to develop this type of analysis for each SBU as data becomes available.

The portfolio is reasonably well balanced at present. There are no services in the liabilities quadrant. We shall need to start thinking about another new business idea fairly soon in order to keep a 'flow' going. We need more revenue from existing cash generators so that we can invest in the high performers and new business ideas. The implications are that we review our pricing and look at ways of saving on costs.

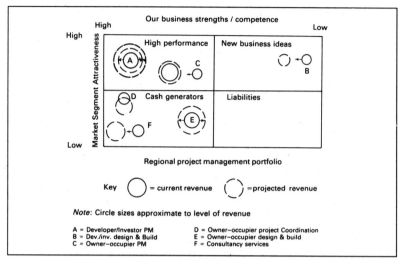

Figure III.8  *Portfolio analysis*

*Marketing objectives and strategies*
Objectives are to increase income from £2.57m to £10.5m over the next 3 years, while at the same time growing net profits from £0.52m to £2.8m. These increases will come from existing business, first, via the following.

Regional project management – objectives
● To increase income from £1.2m to £2.2m over the next 3 years.
● To increase average project size by 25 per cent over that period.
● Each project manager to start two new projects per year.
● Opening of new regional offices or acquisition of existing company will be reviewed throughout the planning period.

Construction management – objectives
● To increase income from £1.07m to £1.8m over the next 3 years.
● Focusing on commercial owner–occupiers and developers in the South East.
● One additional project required each year over the total managed in previous year. Average project value to increase by 10 per cent pa minimum.

Special projects – objectives
● To increase income from £0.3m to £1.3m over the next 3 years.
● To treble the number of contacts made with potential clients each year and improve conversion rate by 25 per cent.

- Average contract value to increase by 10 per cent pa minimum.

New business should increase in the following ways.

Manufacturing process projects – objectives
- To initiate the business by $t+1$ and to earn revenue of £1.9m over the next 2 years.
- Focus on small/medium sized projects in order to gain quick results and demonstrate a track record.

Major projects – objectives
- Starting in $t+1$, to earn revenue of £3.3m over the next 2 years.
- Focus on developers and investors.
- Look for opportunities in public sector.

Long-term strategies beyond the 3-year plan
Build on the expertise we will have developed in terms of planning procedures, systems, quality procedures and staff to lead into new growth market segments. These are likely to be:

Table III.24 The marketing mix

| Strategies | Regional project management | Construction management | Special projects | Manufacturing process projects | Major projects |
|---|---|---|---|---|---|
| Market share | Increase | Increase | Increase | Establish | Establish |
| Promotion | Rely on face-to-face selling skills and developing good personal relationships with clients. Indirect promotion will focus on press releases about success stories, articles in journals and presentations at conferences, etc. Any promotional material will have to be high quality, and consistent with our image. | | | | |
| Price | High end of range | High end of range | High end of range | Competitive for entry | Competitive for entry |
| Product | Increase product surround and provide added value for money | | | Experiment with 'most acceptable' product | |
| Place | Regional representation will be provided whenever possible to establish closeness to clients. This might entail opening new offices in the UK and Europe. | | | | |
| Develop-ments | Develop USPs re value mgmt. Establish letter data re costs and prices. | Consider use of joint-venture approach with suitable partners. | Develop USPs re value mgmt. | Maximize profile with suitable launch. Sales campaigns into target industries. | Maximize profile with suitable launch. Consider acquisition strategy from early days. |

- Large design and build projects (UK and Europe).
- Direct development of property (UK and Europe).
- Major manufacturing process projects (worldwide).

*Marketing strategies, i.e. the marketing mix*
The marketing mix is covered in Table III.24.

*Developing value management*
The project manager's task is two-fold: to manage the physical construction chain and to manage the value-added chain. See Figure III.9.

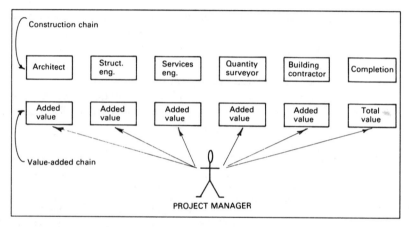

Figure III.9    *Task of project manager*

It is not from the completion of the project that we earn anything. It is the *total added value* from which we earn our profits and reputation.

Added value will accrue from the project manager's ability to reduce costs (in real terms) and to save time. For example, a day saved at an early stage of the chain might lead to many being saved at the later stages of the project, which in turn could dramatically alter the whole cost structure of the construction, both for the client and ourselves.

There must be regular reappraisals of our current working procedures by all project managers and teams in order that we can improve upon the value-added chain.

*Criteria for acquisition*
Should the growth of the project management market outstrip our capabilities to meet demand, we shall need to consider acquiring existing businesses. However, in order to be a genuine asset, such a purchase should meet these criteria.

The company will:

- Have a good reputation in the industry.
- Add to our collective experience, owing to its track record and/or its contacts.
- Provide us with advantageous geographical coverage.
- Provide expertise in terms of its operating systems and procedures, and/or staff.
- Have the financial resources to share in the investment costs of technical development, sales and marketing, and staff training.

For us to be certain we are making a good investment we shall need to:

- Research and monitor our competition, both in the UK and abroad.
- Prioritize the above criteria.
- Select from the competition those which best meet our requirements.
- Identify the mutuality of our objectives and assess the synergistic potential from acquisition.
- Have a short-list of potential candidates.
- Plan a suitable campaign, which will maximize goodwill and a trouble-free integration.

Acquisition might also be considered as a solution to overcoming skill shortages in the short term. In this instance care should be taken that too much extraneous 'baggage' is not taken on board at the same time.

# Moritaki Computers (UK) Ltd

*Background information*

The company was set up 4 years ago by the parent organization, which is in Tokyo. In total the group employs just over 100 people, with approximately half of them based in London.

Between them the two companies provide an international computer consultancy, specializing in the installation, enhancement and support of corporate accounting systems. Both units operate virtually autonomously in terms of seeking new business. Territorially, the London office deals with the northern hemisphere and Tokyo the southern. Although the London office is expected to focus its activities primarily on Europe, it does have a small sales office in New York.

Primarily the target customers are large international companies that continually invest in their management information systems. The Tokyo office already has a client base that includes five of the largest Japanese companies.

The company specializes in the Cassandra (Comprehensive Accounting Spread Sheet and Revenue Analysis) financial accounting system, which is supplied by its producer, Genesis Inc. from California, U.S.A. In addition, there is a systems development group, and multi-user hardware is also supplied.

The total group turnover is expected to be in the order of £3m this year, with London accounting for about 60 per cent of the total.

However, the Managing Director in London was both pleased about the trading success of the young company and yet worried. He knew that his sales team were good at spotting new opportunities as they arose, but could see that there was a danger of a proliferation of products and markets. Indeed there seemed to be a general lack of focus for the company. It was tending to be reactive to the market rather than proactive.

This line of thinking prompted the MD to recruit a Marketing Director, who was given this initial brief:

1  Define a strategy for the company as it moves through a period of rapid expansion and change.
2  Establish some marketing objectives for the company.
3  Lay down some compatible strategies for all our products and services within each of the major market segments in which we compete.
4  Design a framework against which the directors can evaluate and sensibly judge a wide range of marketing opportunities that are uncovered by the sales force.

What follows is the 3-year marketing plan developed by the new Marketing Director for Moritaki Computers (UK) Ltd.

*Moritaki Computers (UK) Ltd – 3-year marketing plan*

Corporate mission
1   To provide a complete service in the design, enhancement, support and development of corporate accounting systems across the major industrial centres of the world.
2   To seek sustained growth through operating with high margins and re-investing a substantial part of our profits. Our profit goal should never be less than 12.5 per cent (after tax and interest charges.
3   To provide a professional service that generates quality solutions to client problems and maintains a high level of customer service.
4   To encourage our staff to use their initiative by giving them responsibility and control over their own spheres of work, and rewarding them according to their contribution to the business.
5   To avoid any business activity that is peripheral and not consistent with our core business. In doing this we expect to double our turnover over the next 3 years.
6   To keep the company privately owned.

Market review
It is possible to describe several key identifying characteristics that typify Moritaki customers:

● They have high expectations of their systems and demand systems capable of providing comprehensive management information about their business activities.
● They are above average in sophistication in their approach to computerization.
● They are perhaps installing a computerized accounting system for the second or third time.
● They are large companies with specialist financial and accounting functions.
● They are faced with multi-currency or other difficult reporting requirements.
● They consider their investment in information systems in terms of their strategic value to the company as well as cost benefits.
● They demand high quality and superior support services.

The following three market segments would appear to offer us the best opportunities for providing complete business systems, consistent with the above customer profile.

1 *European multi-national companies.* These offer the prospect of multiple installations on an international scale.
2 *Large UK firms with complex currency/information requirements.* Our expertise and ability to enhance the product gives considerable scope in this segment.
3 *Japanese multi-national companies that are clients of Moritaki in Japan, but with a presence in the northern hemisphere.* Introductions are easy and logistically it is better to service these clients from London rather than Japan.

Competition and company image
A survey was conducted by 'phoning a number of existing and potential client companies:

(a) *How well is Mortaki known?* From a sample of twenty typical client companies selected at random, we got the results listed in Table III.25. Compared with our major competitors we are one of the least well-known suppliers (together with Competitor D). In contrast everyone has heard of Competitor G.

*Table III.25* Customer knowledge of companies

|  | Percentage |
|---|---|
| Competitor A | 75% |
| Competitor B | 95% |
| Competitor C | 60% |
| Competitor D | 50% |
| Competitor E | 65% |
| Competitor F | 80% |
| Competitor G | 100% |
| Moritaki (UK) | 55% |

(b) *Quality of the product.* From a sample of eighteen users, scoring 1–10 points (10 = highest quality) we got the data in Table III.26. We can see that the Cassandra system is perceived to be superior in quality to competing systems by users who are in a position to make a comparison.

*Table III.26* Customer's opinion of quality

|  | AV score |
|---|---|
| System W | 6.3 |
| System X | 5.8 |
| System Y | 7.9 |
| System Z | 6.7 |
| Cassandra | 9.2 |

(c) *Marketing ability*. From a sample of twenty companies where we are known, with scoring between 1 (low) and 10 (high), we obtained the results shown in Table III.27. Competitor G is seen to have the highest level of marketing ability, whereas we have the lowest average score.

*Table III.27* Marketing ability

|  | Average score |
|---|---|
| Competitor A | 5.4 |
| Competitor B | 6.2 |
| Competitor C | 7.8 |
| Competitor D | 4.8 |
| Competitor E | 5.0 |
| Competitor F | 5.5 |
| Competitor G | 9.4 |
| Moritaki (UK) | 4.5 |

Little information is known about competitors, but on the basis of some admittedly rather crude surveys it appears that:

- We are little known outside our existing bank of clients.
- Our product is the best on the market.
- We are not perceived as having much marketing ability.

This helps to explain why 65 per cent of our business is either from repeat sales or referrals from existing customers. Useful though this is, we will need to be capable of breaking out of our existing customer network if we are to achieve the corporate objectives of doubling our turnover over the next 3 years.

Market positioning
It is possible to define our existing position and determine our reposi-tioning strategy by using the 'map' shown in Figure III.10. The new

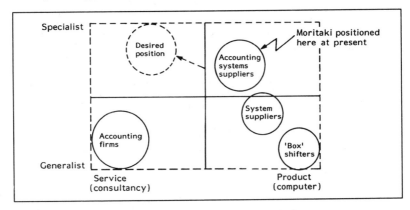

Figure III.10  *Marketing positioning*

position is more consistent with the corporate objective of being a professional, specialist, consultancy company, providing a high level of customer service.

Marketing environment
The foreseeable threats and their potential to damage us are best described in Table III.28.

Table III.28   Threat analysis

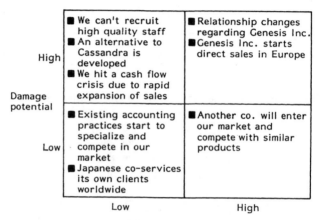

```
              |  ■ We can't recruit      | ■ Relationship changes
              |    high quality staff    |   regarding Genesis Inc.
              |  ■ An alternative to     | ■ Genesis Inc. starts
      High    |    Cassandra is          |   direct sales in Europe
              |    developed             |
              |  ■ We hit a cash flow    |
              |    crisis due to rapid   |
Damage        |    expansion of sales    |
potential     |──────────────────────────┼──────────────────────────
              |  ■ Existing accounting   | ■ Another co. will enter
              |    practices start to    |   our market and
              |    specialize and        |   compete with similar
      Low     |    compete in our        |   products
              |    market                |
              |  ■ Japanese co-services  |
              |    its own clients       |
              |    worldwide             |

                    Low                          High
                    Likelihood of occurrence
```

Equally there are a number of opportunities, as described in Table III.29.

Table III.29   Opportunity analysis

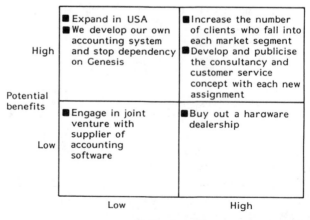

```
              |  ■ Expand in USA          | ■ Increase the number
              |  ■ We develop our own     |   of clients who fall into
              |    accounting system      |   each market segment
      High    |    and stop dependency    | ■ Develop and publicise
              |    on Genesis             |   the consultancy and
              |                           |   customer service
              |                           |   concept with each new
Potential     |                           |   assignment
benefits      |───────────────────────────┼──────────────────────────
              |  ■ Engage in joint        | ■ Buy out a hardware
              |    venture with           |   dealership
              |    supplier of            |
      Low     |    accounting             |
              |    software               |

                    Low                          High
                    Ability to achieve
```

Product plans and analyses
Since the organization could be said to have the layout shown in Figure
III.11, what follows are individual analyses of the three component parts
that comprise Moritaki (UK) Ltd.

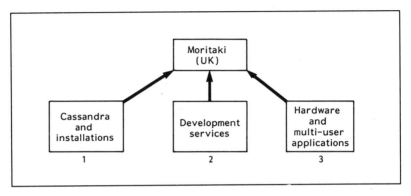

Figure III.11   *Organizational layout*

*Cassandra system*
Our experience so far suggests the following:

● We have the best available product in the market.
● We have a very high level of experience with this system and a track
  record of successful installations and satisfied clients.
● Our development staff understands the open architecture of the
  product and can identify cross-selling opportunities for enhancement
  services.
● We have a special relationship with the producers, Genesis, who
  provide us with customer leads.
● The product has a life-cycle of at least another two years, because of
  the conservative nature of the client companies and its relative lack
  of penetration in the market.

Sales have followed the pattern in Figure III.12 up to now. We need
to:

● Monitor sales to get better at establishing life-cycle trends.
● Monitor competitor activity.
● Start thinking about the system to succeed Cassandra.

Critical installation factors that generate success
Ranked in order to importance they are:

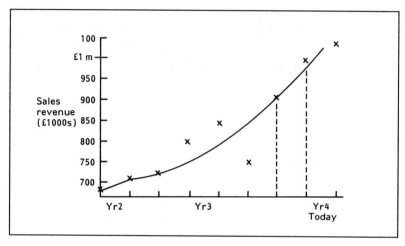

Figure III.12   *Sales pattern*

1 Ability to provide a complete system including installation.
2 Ability to understand client's needs and talk in his language.
3 Demonstrable technical competence, e.g. track record.
4 Value for money, e.g. valued added or cost savings.
5 Ability to customize product to meet special requirements.
6 High level of service and customer support.

SWOT analysis

*Strengths*
● Our technical knowledge and expertise.
● Accounting background.
● Track record.
● Relationship with Genesis.

*Weaknesses*
● High perceived level of charges.
● Not well known in market.
● Dependency on Genesis.
● Lack of customer service skills/consulting skills.

*Opportunities*
● Expand level of consultancy with each installation.
● Add other services to enhance system.

*Threats*
● Not getting right quality staff as we expand.
● Genesis might use own sales team in Europe.
● Maintaining standards with rapid expansion.

Key issues
- We must focus on our 'customer services' not our 'product'.
- Our high perceived level of fees is because we are associated with 'computer companies', not professional service companies.
- We need to develop selling and customer service skills in installation staff, thereby generating more leads and business.
- We must maintain the high quality of installations.
- We need to keep Genesis out of Europe by persuasion.

Our objectives are shown in Table III.30.

*Table III.30*  Objectives

|  | Now | + 3 yrs |
|---|---|---|
| Turnover (£m) | £1.1 | £1.98 |
| Contribution (£k) | £105 | £175 |
| Growth | x1 | x1.8 |

Key assumptions
- No system superior to Cassandra comes on the market in the next 3 years.
- The relationship with Genesis stays cordial.
- There is no worldwide trade recession.

Strategies
- Present our range of products and services as a complete corporate accounting system.
- Add as much value as possible to each installation.
- More meetings with clients before installation in order to:
  (a) Explore all accounting and systems issues.
  (b) Create in the customer's mind the distinction between the software and the final completed system.

Pricing
Our current charges are 20–30 per cent higher than our main competitors', and have probably inhibited our level of business in the past. Our proposed market positioning can sustain this price differential, but as an interim measure we will need to carry out some research to find out:

- Customer perceptions about our fee levels.
- What the market will bear.
- How we can adopt a pricing strategy that will be consistent with our changing image.

Promotional strategy
We should get the company better known in general by:

- Getting articles etc. into clients' trade journals.
- Running seminars about specific problems that will interest potential clients.
- Re-evaluating our existing promotional materials and upgrading where necessary.
- Exhibiting at one or two prestigious venues.
- Investing in a limited advertising campaign.

Because of our relative lack of experience in the visual impact of designing promotional materials, exhibitions and advertising, outside consultants will have to be used.

Sales strategy
- Recognize that every contact with a client is a sales opportunity.
- Train all installation staff in selling and customer service skills.
- Ensure that installation staff are aware of all other products and services and can sell 'through the range'.
- Develop a client contact plan as a means of improving our relationships with clients before and after a sale.

Product strategy
- Develop installation checklists to ensure consistent standards.
- Standardize pre- and post-installation evaluation checks.

*Development services*
These services have the following advantages:

- Can provide bespoke systems to extend the facilities of Cassandra.
- Use COBOL, same as Cassandra, hence no additional learning required by clients.
- Provide database requirements for clients.
- Several similar bespoke systems have been amalgamated into specific 'products', which include:
- 'Loans and overdraft' system.
- 'Futures investment' system.

Critical success factors for development work
These are ranked in order of importance:

1   Services outmatching the clients' internal services in terms of charges and completion times.

2  Talking the clients' language.
3  Being able to demonstrate a track record.
4  Availability, when client has a problem.

SWOT analysis

*Strengths*
● Very high technical skills.
● Intimate knowledge of Cassandra system.
● Staff have financial background.
● Have accumulated a 'portfolio' of bespoke solutions to many client problems.

*Weaknesses*
● Tend to be more interested in the technical problems than the client's problems.
● Lack of customer awareness.
● Lack of co-ordination regarding similar projects.
● Lack of control/project management on large projects.
● No promotional material for this service.

*Opportunities*
● To exploit some of the 'bespoke' systems.

*Threats*
● Recruiting and keeping quality staff is a problem.
● Quality will suffer if department is overloaded.

Key issues to be addressed
● How to get better control and co-ordination of projects at all stages.
● Getting better customer service skills.
● Recruitment, training and rewards package for development staff to be improved.

Our objectives are shown in Table III.31.

Table III.31   Objectives

|                   | Now    | + 3 yrs |
|-------------------|--------|---------|
| Turnover (£m)     | £ 400  | £ 800   |
| Contribution (£k) | £ 38   | £ 79    |
| Growth            | x1     | x2      |

Assumptions
We must assume that there will be no crashes in the financial markets.

Pricing strategy
In order that we maximize our profits, there are two considerations:

(a) Our prices are competitive.

(b) We do not run over the time allowed for each project.

The better the record of delivering on time, the more we can justify above-average prices.

The whole situation regarding prices for development needs reviewing. Current market prices have been distorted by the inclusion of the fees of 'one-man bands' who could not tackle most of the projects we undertake.

Promotional strategy
The main promotional thrust for Cassandra and installations will also publicize our development services. In addition staff will be trained in selling and customer service skills.

Product strategy
- Develop a 'house-style' in terms of design, coding and testing so that a consistent quality and appearance is perceived by clients.
- We must continually take full advantage of the latest developments in both software and hardware.

*Hardware and multi-user applications*
- Two-thirds of our installations are integrated with some form of PC network.
- New and existing machines can be linked via a network.
- Increasing interest in market re multi-user systems.
- We supply maintenance and support contracts.

Critical success factors
These are ranked in order of importance:

1 Confidence client places in technical skills and abilities of the consultant.
2 Ability to provide general advice as well as the mainstream topic.
3 Speed of response and back-up services.
4 Prices of products and services.
5 Selling and customer contact skills.

SWOT analysis

*Strengths*
- Technically astute.
- Customer-orientated.

*Weaknesses*
- We are small compared with specialist firms in this part of the market.
- Limited on dealerships with major equipment manufacturers.
- Outdated promotional material.

*Opportunities*
- Growing demand for networks.
- Our preferred multi-user system is becoming very popular and could be promoted.
- Become agent for overseas equipment manufacturer.

*Threats*
- Larger companies enjoy economies of scale.
- Dependent on sales of Cassandra to generate business.
- Competition is getting fiercer in this market.

Key issues to be addressed
- Targets to be set for non-Cassandra work.
- More promotion effort to get known in market.
- Capitalization on growing demand for networks and multi-user applications.

Our objectives are shown in Table III.32.

*Table III.32* Objectives

|  | Now | + 3 yrs |
|---|---|---|
| Turnover (£m) | £250 | £720 |
| Contribution (£k) | £24 | £66 |
| Growth | x1 | x2.9 |

Assumptions
- Current growth trends for networks and multi-user systems will continue.
- Sales for Cassandra reach their projected levels.

Pricing strategy
We need to focus on 'added value' not 'cheapness'. We provide very good products, excellent and impartial technical advice, above-average installation and maintenance services, a fast response to client problems and a flexible approach. The product is only part of this 'package'; therefore we will avoid discounting as practised by the 'box shifters'.

In the short term (up to one year) prices will stay the same. Thereafter we will push to charge the highest the market will bear, in line with our publicity and company image campaigns.

Promotion strategy
- Develop promotional materials.
- Set realistic sales targets for non-Cassandra-linked work.
- Ensure that staff can sell 'through the range'.

Product strategy
- Keep abreast of all new developments.
- Standardize as much as possible on configurations, installation checks, pre- and post-installation tests.
- Develop closer ties with major hardware suppliers.

# Houston marketing plan
## *Based on a real marketing plan in the airline industry, 1984/5 to 1989*

The data and information presented here have been disguised and some parts removed in order to preserve confidentiality. However, although not all the extracts chosen relate to each other, sufficient detail has been provided to enable you to appreciate what a complete Strategic Marketing Plan looks like.

*Market review*
The city of Houston is dominated by oil production. In the early 1980s, it was at the bottom of a recession, with full recovery not expected until 1990. The economy was unstable and very volatile, due to the glut of oil in the open market and the fall in the price per barrel.

Totally dependent on the oil industry, Houston did not diversify sufficiently in other industries to make up for the deficit of the oil-related activities.

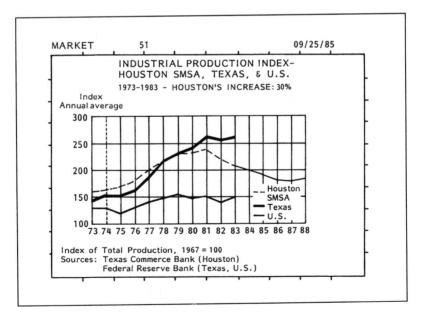

Figure III.13

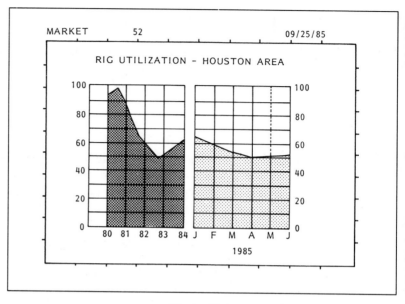

Figure III.14

The Industrial Production Index (Figure III.13) was well above the US average, and it used to be above the Texas average, until 1980. In the early 1980s it was in sharp decline; it fell from an index of 240 in 1981 to 210 in 1983, and continued to fall for the next 2 years before it stabilized.

Rig utilization was down from almost 100 per cent in 1980/81 to just 50 per cent in 1982/83 (Figure III.14). It increased to some 63 per cent in January 1985 and then dropped again to just over 50 per cent, where it remained. Many large contractors withdrew their fleets from the field, and there were no indications of any improvement. Staff levels and production were reduced accordingly.

Per capita personal income in Houston (Figure III.15) increased from US $4000 in 1971 to US $13,000 in 1981. However, it was down to US $12,500 in 1983/84. It was certainly not expected to grow, as the economy remained unstable and because salary levels had dropped.

From 1974 to 1981 the number of British subsidiaries in the Houston area rose from twenty-five in 1974 to a total of 170 in 1981. It remained static for the next 3 years, and was expected to hold for the next 3 years. Here again, the oil related 'boom' had stopped.

Unemployment in the Houston area never exceeded 4.6 per cent from 1973 until 1981. In 1982 it jumped to 6.7 per cent and in 1983 to 9.3 per cent, which was almost equal to the US average. The unemployment figures for July 1985 showed 7.7 per cent for the state of Texas

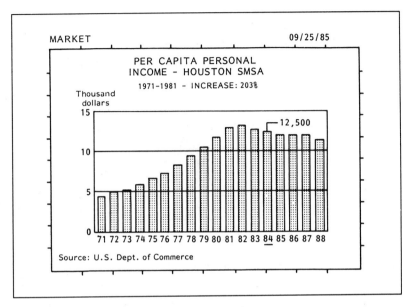

Figure III.15

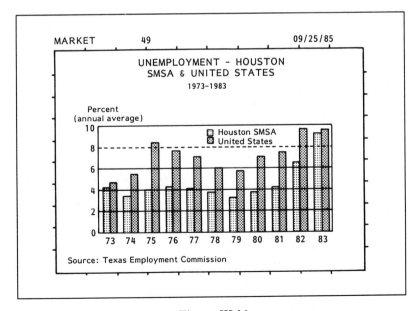

Figure III.16

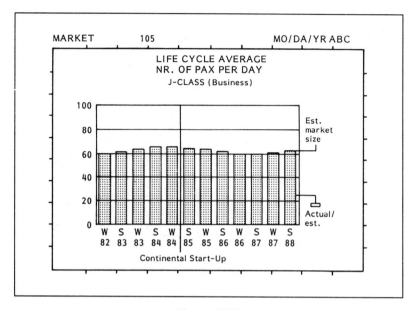

Figure  III.17

*Table III.33* Market growth – Houston total
passengers departing for Europe

|  | No. | % Change |
|---|---|---|
| 1984 | 111,317 | +1 |
| 1983 | 110,211 | −20 |
| 1982 | 136,978 | +13 |
| 1981 | 121,490 | +4 |
| 1980 | 116,710 | +26 |

*Table III.34* Critical success factors

|  | BR | CO | AF | KL | AA | PA | People |
|---|---|---|---|---|---|---|---|
| Non-stop service | A | A | C | B | B | B | C |
| Feed to/from IAH | C | A | C | C | B | B | C |
| Frequency | A | A | B | A | A | B | C |
| Competitive Pricing | B | A | B | B | A | A | A |
| Frequent Traveller | C | A | B | B | A | A | C |
| Image | A | B | B | A | A | B | C |
| Beyond Points | A | C | A | A | B | B | C |
| Widebody 747/Config. | B | B | A | A | B | A | B |

A = Good to excellent.
B = Satisfactory.
C = Bad to non-existent.

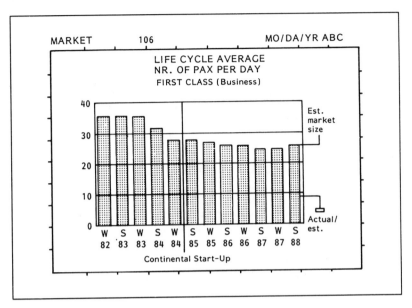

Figure III.18

(up by 1.4 per cent compared with July 1984); in Houston, the unemployment rate over the same 12-month period rose from 7.1 per cent to 8.4 per cent. See Figure III.16.

*Outside influences on airlines*
We are influenced by American political differences with foreign countries, as in the case of Libya. Domestic UK problems can also have adverse effects; for instance, the violence by the English soccer fans in Belgium and racial disturbances such as the riots in Birmingham and other major cities.

The continuous hijacking problem and a series of accidents and incidents have hit the airline industry in general.

The first-class market is small and is in decline, and new carriers have moved in – Continental with daily non-stop services to London Gatwick, and Lufthansa non-stop to Frankfurt, with a high level of service. Because of the increased competition, yields declined quite dramatically for both passenger sales and cargo.

Last, but in no way least, the stronger pound versus the weaker dollar has influenced the flow of traffic to and from the USA.

The number of passengers leaving Houston for Europe, 1980–4, is shown in Table III.33. Figures III.17 and III.18 show average number of passengers per day, 1982–8, in J-class and first class respectively.

Table III.34 shows the CSFs in various airlines' performance.

*Passenger sales*

*Our strengths*

| | F | J | Y |
|---|---|---|---|
| | | *Class* | |
| Reputation and high awareness | X | X | X |
| High standards of service | X | X | |
| Commission levels and relationship with travel agents | X | X | X |
| Punctuality | X | X | X |

*Our weaknesses*

| | F | J | Y |
|---|---|---|---|
| | | *Class* | |
| Small and declining market | X | | |
| One film against two of competitor | X | X | X |
| Congested lounge and no identity | X | | |
| Lack of lounge facilities | | | X |
| Departure time, just after main competitor | X | X | X |
| No frequent traveller incentive | X | X | X |
| 7-abreast seating | | | X |
| Low awareness of BCAL network | X | X | X |
| Lack of executive class Europe/Nigeria | X | X | |
| Lack of capacity European services | | X | X |
| Price perception: more expensive than competitor | | X | X |
| Lack of advance seat selection | | X | X |

*Our opportunities*

| | F | J | Y |
|---|---|---|---|
| | | *Class* | |
| Earlier departure, ahead of competitor | X | X | X |
| Price strategy (2 for 1; winter special) | X | X | |
| Frequent flyer incentive (VAT) | X | X | X |
| Small F-class cabin and 6-abreast in larger J-class cabin | X | X | |
| Meet and greet chauffeur-driven service | X | | |
| Free helicopter service Houston and destination | X | | |
| Own lounge(s) | X | X | |
| Complimentary hotel accommodation London | X | X | |
| New routes to Middle East | | X | X |
| Executive product Europe and Nigeria | X | X | |
| Hobby airport interline potential and new feed (US Air and Pride Air) | X | X | X |
| Beyond London Gatwick – European markets | X | X | X |
| Free rail tickets | X | X | X |
| Advance seat selection | | | X |

| | | | |
|---|---|---|---|
| Through check-in facilities | X | X | X |
| Strong, competitive in-house product | | | X |

| *Our threats* | | *Class* | |
|---|---|---|---|
| | F | J | Y |
| A continuing decline of the market | X | | |
| Improvement of competitor's product | X | X | X |
| Competitor's price strategy (2 for 1) | X | X | X |
| New, larger (747?) equipment by competitor | X | X | X |
| Limitation of the Houston catchment area – lack of feed | X | X | X |
| Currency fluctuations | | | |
| New carriers to/from Europe (SR, SK) | X | X | X |
| Accidents/incidents in industry | | | |
| Unrest and riots in UK | | | |
| London pricing itself out of the market | | | |
| Declining London saturation | | | |
| Competitor's strong in-house products | | | |

(F = First, J = Super Executive, Y = Economy)

*Market segment definition, leisure*

1   Groups – middle income, churches, fraternal, special interest, incentive, student.
2   VFR – individual, $25,000+, ethnic connection.
3   Wholesaler – large travel corporations that buy in bulk based on price/schedules.

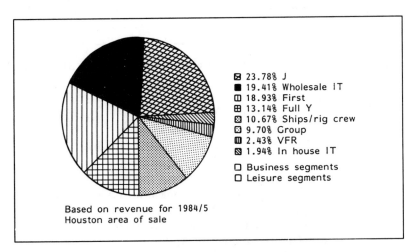

23.78% J
19.41% Wholesale IT
18.93% First
13.14% Full Y
10.67% Ships/rig crew
9.70% Group
2.43% VFR
1.94% In house IT

□ Business segments
□ Leisure segments

Based on revenue for 1984/5
Houston area of sale

Figure III.19   *Total market segments*

4 In-house tour programme – $25,000 (individual income) individual/family units (mainly female).

5 Agency IT – local wholesaler, regional operators trading in limited geographical areas, using only one/two gateways.

Total market segments are illustrated in Figure III.19.

*Houston cargo market*

Table III.35 evaluates market attractiveness, and Table III.36 business strength.

*Table III.35* Market attractiveness evaluation

| Prime tariff | Score | Weighting | Ranking |
|---|---|---|---|
| Market size | 4 | 30 | 1.20 |
| Decline/growth | 4 | 20 | 0.80 |
| Competition | 8 | 15 | 1.20 |
| Yield return | 9 | 20 | 1.80 |
| Sensitivity to price | 7 | 15 | 1.05 |
| | | 100 | 6.05 |

Houston area of sale
Score: 1 = low
10 = high

*Table III.36* Business strength

| Prime tariff | Score | Weighting | Ranking |
|---|---|---|---|
| Market share | 6 | 35 | 2.10 |
| Image | 7 | 10 | 0.70 |
| Profitability | 8 | 25 | 2.00 |
| Strength/ | 6 | 15 | 0.90 |
| Growth to B-CAL | 7 | 10 | 0.70 |
| | | 100 | 6.40 |

Portfolio matrices are illustrated in Figures III.20 and III.21.

Assumptions
- 747 Combi on IAH.
- ABZ oil market continues to grow.
- No political upheaval in Nigeria or Libya.
- Development of European trucking.
- Larger aircraft on European routes.
- ARAMCO contract is implemented and maintained.
- 747 Combi on DXB-HKG.
- Approval on new Middle East route.
- DC10 aircraft replace A310.
- Continued decline in yield.

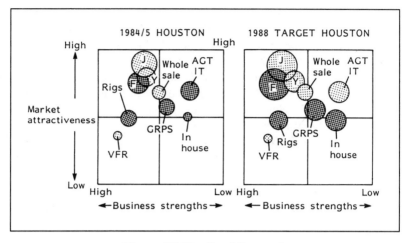

Figure III.20   *Portfolio matrix*

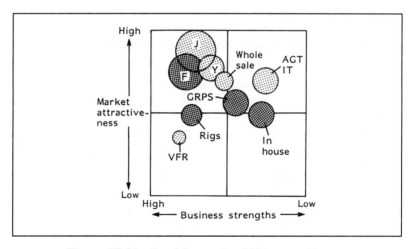

Figure III.21   *Portfolio matrix, 1988 target Houston*

- Continued price war.
- Currency fluctuations diminish.
- Development of commercial market.

Key factors for success
- 747 Combi.
- European trucking and/or larger aircraft.
- Commercial cargo sales representative (cost £32,142 PA)
- Purchase agents/agent.

Objectives
- Maintain UK market share at 60 per cent and increase to 70 per cent (based on tonnage) for 77.5 tonnage gain and revenue increase of £74,000.
- Develop offline traffic with purchase of agents – agent for initial increase 34.8 tonnage and revenue gain £69,600.
- Develop and penetrate European market. Present market share less than 1 per cent. Estimated gain of 46.4 tonnage and revenue increase £52,000.
- Introduce 747 Combi for an increase of 1,250.0 tonnage and revenue gain of £1,300,000.

Strategies

*Promotion service-related*
- Appoint commercial cargo sales representative (est. cost $45,000 – £32,142).
- Enhance our customer servicing.
- Obtain training in Houston oil business and related products shipped to acquire increased commercial business.

*Distribution-related*
- Develop direct mail campaign.
- Obtain more effective statistical information.
- Develop drop stations for cargo in New Orleans and San Antonio.

*Product-related*
- Introduction of 747 Combi. on Houston route.
- Introduction of European trucking.
- Improved transfer times through LGW/LHR.
- Purchase agents/agent.

*Price-related*
- Continue to develop more competitive commission structures to meet market demands.
- Maintain competitive pricing on European routes.
- Introduce container pricing into Saudi Arabia.

Figure III.22 illustrates Ansoff Matrix for Houston cargo products.

*Objectives and strategy*
The objectives are to maintain and increase share of the business travel market segments. The strategy with effect from Spring 1986, is to introduce a Boeing 747-Combi on the Houston route with the following configuration and product enhancement.

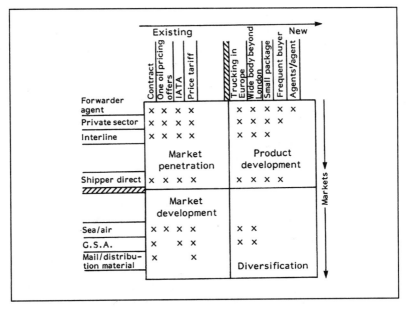

Figure III.22 *Ansoff matrix – Houston cargo products*

*First Class (F)*
Objectives:
to hold/increase market share in declining but attractive market.
Strategies:
(a) Reduce size of cabin to 16/18 seats
(b) Introduce a 'meet & greet' chauffeur service
    in Houston                                                                    £300,000
(c) Offer complimentary London hotel accommodation
    – 2 night package                                                             £206,000
(d) Advertising and promotion of these two services                              £75,000
(e) Open BR's own First Class lounge                                             Capital
(f) Introduce a bonus point system for frequent
    FC pax whereby they receive a certain number
    of points for either gifts or free travel                                     Corporate

   TOTAL COST                                                                     £581,000

First Class revenue potential 900 r/t incremental
pax increase plus retention of existing market share:
(2.5 pax per flight) × £2250 RT yield ×
number of flights (360) =                                                         £2,025,000
F Class gross contribution                                                        £1,444,000

*Super Executive Class* (*J*)
Objectives:
to increase market share in an increasingly attractive market.
Strategies:
(a)  6-abreast seating
(b)  Larger cabin (approximately 40–45 seats)
(c)  Offer complimentary London hotel
        accommodation – one night package
        $25 \times £75 \times 360 =$                                                   £241,000
(d)  Offer use of Continental's lounge
TOTAL COST                                                                   £241,000

Super Executive revenue potential 1260 pax:
(3.5 pax per flight) $\times$ £1428 RT yield $\times$ 360 =        £1,799,280
J Class Gross Contribution                                        £1,558,280

*Economy Class* (*Y*)
Objectives: to hold/increase market share in a declining market
Strategy: introduce advance seating selection

Revenue/economy potential 900 pax (2.5 pax
increase per flight): Y Class Gross Contribution            £636,000

Revenue potential:
F Class                                                                      £2,025,000
J Class                                                                      £1,799,000
Y Class                                                                        £636,000

TOTAL                                                                        £4,460,000

Gap analysis
Figures III.23 and III.24 illustrate gap analyses for load and revenue
respectively.

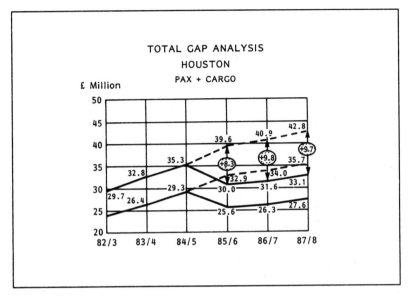

Figure III.23   *Total gap analysis, Houston, pax + cargo*

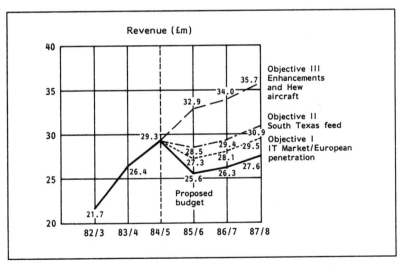

Figure III.24   *Houston gap analysis, revenue (£ millions)*

# Index